1991

THE

REFERENCE

SHELF

AFFIRMATIVE ACTION

edited by DONALD ALTSCHILLER

THE REFERENCE SHELF

Volume 63 Number 3

THE H. W. WILSON COMPANY

New York   1991

THE REFERENCE SHELF

The books in this series contain reprints of articles, excerpts from books, and addresses on current issues and social trends in the United States and other countries. There are six separately bound numbers in each volume, all of which are generally published in the same calendar year. One number is a collection of recent speeches; each of the others is devoted to a single subject and gives background information and discussion from various points of view, concluding with a comprehensive bibliography that contains books and pamphlets and abstracts of additional articles on the subject. Books in the series may be purchased individually or on subscription.

Library of Congress Cataloging-in-Publication Data

Main entry under title:

Affirmative action / edited by Donald Altschiller.
    p.   cm — (The Reference shelf ; v. 63, no. 3)
    ISBN 0-8242-0813-7
    1. Affirmative action programs—Law and legislation—United
States.   I. Altschiller, Donald.   II. Series.
KF4755.5.A75A38   1991
342.73'0873—dc20
[347.302873]   91-14134
                                                                                   CIP

Cover: Students at Harvard University march in protest to demand an increase in minority faculty hiring.
Photo: Ira Wyman

Printed in the United States of America

CONTENTS

140,960

3

IV. WHITE REACTION

V. PERSONAL REFLECTIONS

BIBLIOGRAPHY

PREFACE

In 1961 President Kennedy issued Executive Order 10925, requiring federal contractors to take "affirmative action" to recruit workers on a nondiscriminatory basis. Since then, few domestic issues have been so controversial or have inspired such heated debate. What exactly is affirmative action? Often the answer is dependent upon where one stands on the issue. Myrl Duncan of Washburn University's School of Law in Topeka, Kansas explains: "The term refers to "public and private programs designed to equalize hiring and admission opportunities for historically disadvantaged groups by taking into consideration those very characteristics which have been used to deny them equal treatment."

Historically, the Supreme Court has mirrored society's attitudes on race, equality, and social justice. At times, this has resulted in decisions like *Dred Scott* and the infamous *Plessy v. Ferguson*, which established the "separate but equal" doctrine and solidified the Jim Crow practices of segregation throughout the south and in many northern cities. At other times, as in the 1954 landmark case of *Brown v. Board of Education*, the Court has stood as a beacon for those seeking racial equality. The Supreme Court has been a major arena in the debate over affirmative action.

The first section of this compilation contains articles that describe the legal aspects of affirmative action, focusing especially on recent Supreme Court decisions and on legal redress for those who feel they have been discriminated against.

The second section deals with the prospects of affirmative action in the work place. "Managing Diversity" is rapidly becoming the catchphrase in American business and industry, as changing demographics, consumer needs, and competition from abroad force companies to develop new and innovative affirmative action programs.

The next section discusses the impact of affirmative action on student admissions and faculty recruitment in America's colleges and universities. The articles explore the challenges faced by college administrators who seek to establish a diversified university while promoting fairness and maintaining excellence.

The fourth section deals with a range of attitudes among whites towards affirmative action.

The final section features the personal reflections of a diverse group of individuals on how affirmative action has affected their lives.

The Editor wishes to thank the publishers who have granted permission to reprint their material in this compilation.

Donald Altschiller

January 1991

I. THE LEGAL DIMENSIONS OF AFFIRMATIVE ACTION

EDITOR'S INTRODUCTION

Although affirmative action policies have provoked philosophical and political debate, the primary battleground has been in the courts, most importantly, the Supreme Court. It is to this body that interested and affected parties have turned for solutions and answers to all-too difficult questions. In various decisions over the years the Court has given a boost to both proponents and opponents of affirmative action. At times it has appeared schizophrenic, simultaneously endorsing affirmative action while severely limiting its scope.

In the first selection, "Equality of Opportunity or Equality of Results," Clarence Pendleton and Douglas Huron, each writing a part of the article, address the pros and cons of affirmative action and the real intent of the Civil Rights Act of 1964. The second article, written by Samuel Rabinove, offers a conspectus and brief analysis of recent Supreme Court rulings that affect affirmative action. The final selection is a reprint of an article by Supreme Court Justice Thurgood Marshall from *USA Today* magazine. Disturbed by what he calls the Court's retrenchment of the civil rights agenda, he warns that the trend of recent rulings on affirmative action may be a harbinger of things to come.

EQUALITY OF OPPORTUNITY OR EQUALITY OF RESULTS[1]

Opportunity

It has been more than 20 years since the Civil Rights Act of 1964 was passed, and the debate over what Congress intended still rages.

[1]Reprint of an article by Clarence M. Pendleton, former chairman of the U.S. Commission on Civil Rights, and Douglas Huron, former senior trial lawyer with the Justice Department, Civil Rights Division. *Human Rights,* a publication of the American Bar Association, 19 1, Fall 1985. Reprinted with permission. Mr. Pendleton wrote the first section, "Opportunity"; and Mr. Huron wrote the concluding section, "Results."

7

During the last 21 years, the question has remained: Was the intent of Congress to provide equality of opportunity or equality of results?

For 84 days, the longest debate in its history, the Senate tried to resolve the issue in 1964. We still have not answered the question.

Many leading civil rights organizations at that time, led by Senator Hubert Humphrey, argued the equality of opportunity side. Humphrey assured his colleagues time and again that group preferences were not to be tolerated.

There is nothing in Title VII of the bill, he insisted, "that will give any power to the (Equal Employment Opportunity) Commission or to any court to require hiring, firing or promotion of employees in order to meet a racial 'quota' or to achieve a certain racial balance. That bugaboo has been brought up a dozen times; but it is nonexistent."

The opposition believed that, despite the intent of the bill, the effect would be to insure equality of results, as interpreted by the enforcing agencies of government.

The act was passed to substantiate the rights of blacks. However, the bill's language insisted that race, color, religion, and national origin were to limit no one's rights.

The act followed the language and spirit of the 13th, 14th, and 15th amendments to the Constitution. It spoke of "citizens, individuals, and persons," not blacks, not Hispanics, native Americans, Asians, or any other group that might be subject to discrimination.

It seemed as though Justice John Marshall Harlan's famous dissent in *Plessy v. Ferguson* would be the law at last: "In view of the Constitution, in the eye of the law, there is in this country no superior, dominant ruling class of citizens. There is no caste here. Our Constitution is color-blind, and neither knows nor tolerates classes among its citizens.

"In respect of civil rights, all citizens are equal before the law. The humblest is the peer of the most powerful. The law regards man as man, and takes no account of his surroundings or of his color when his civil rights as guaranteed by the supreme law of the Land are involved."

Americans thought the eloquent words spoken by Dr. Martin Luther King Jr. from the steps of the Lincoln Memorial were cast in stone. All people, he said, were "to be judged by the content of their character not by the color of their skin."

One would be sadly and grossly mistaken to believe that a color-blind society has been obtained. The implementation and enforcement of this law, as columnist George Will once described, succeeded in dividing "the majestic national river into little racial and ethnic creeks."

The United States, Will wrote, became "less a nation than an angry menagerie of factions scrambling for preference."

The massive societal consensus that demanded passage of the Civil Rights Act of 1964 began to break down in the 1970s. New legislation and an executive order required increased attention to race and ethnicity in hiring by any private or public employer that received federal aid or was subject to government regulation.

It was now required to count how many minorities were recruited, interviewed, trained, hired, admitted, served or enrolled.

Twenty years later, it is still necessary "to count noses" to determine if there is discrimination.

That equality of opportunity so ardently fought for and won in 1964 has given way to equality of results through such bureaucratic devices as fair share, proportional representation, special preferences, quotas, goals, timetables, and set-asides.

Today, many blacks believe that the laws were passed to ensure only their civil rights, and that blacks are due a special preference from the government to make up for the despicable institution of slavery. They sincerely believe that the government has not yet made up for past atrocities.

This is where I part company with some of my people. I believe that blacks were only due the granting of equal status, equal protection. I also believe that many of the laws and court decisions that occurred since 1964 were necessary to reassert the constitutional guarantees expressed by the 13th, 14th, and 15th amendments.

Insistence on group preference is a role reversal. Those who marched, struggled and died for equality now want separation.

In enforcing the Civil Rights Act, the government perpetuated and worsened the situation with a myriad of artificial allotments, considered incentives to assist and propel minorities into America's mainstream.

Those artificial allotments included goals, timetables, quotas and other numerical devices imposed by government to suit its notion of how society should be organized—a society where a person's standing is determined by pigment, ethnicity or gender.

Allocating social benefits on the basis of race or gender has led to bitterness and disharmony. Economist Thomas Sowell expressed a cause for concern when he stated, "There is much reason to fear the harm that (a racial preference) is doing to its supposed beneficiaries, and still more reason to fear the long-run consequences of polarizing the nation. Resentments do not accumulate indefinitely without consequences."

The U.S. Commission on Civil Rights is studying the long- and short-term consequences of these artificial allotments. Some of the issues under study are:

• *Incomes of Americans: ethnic, racial and sex differences.* The commission is examining how employment discrimination, schooling and work experience have affected income differences between men, women, racial and ethnic groups since the 1940s.

• *Affirmative action in higher education.* Techniques used by universities to increase minority and female representation among students and faculty members will be studied, along with success rates. The study will also assess the effect of affirmative action on different types of institutions and their student bodies, faculties, curricula, standards of admission, grading, progress, and graduation.

• *Voluntary and involuntary methods of achieving school desegregation.* We are studying how busing, magnet schools, open enrollment, and special attendance schools have worked to achieve integration in up to 40 sites. We want to know how long integration was achieved and effects on the communities involved.

• *State and local civil rights enforcement.* The commission is evaluating how well state and local vocational rehabilitation agencies are enforcing civil rights.

• *Redistricting and minorities.* The commission has started a study of redistricting by state and local governments in order to comply with the one-person, one-vote principle for apportioning representation following 1980 census data.

We want to know whether redistricting plans dilute the voting strength of minorities in violation of the Voting Rights Act and the Constitution. We are also examining the effects of various districting plans on the opportunity of minorities to effectively participate in the political process.

• *Comparable worth.* The notion that equal pay should be given not only for equal work, but for jobs deemed comparable in the skills, knowledge and ability they require has emerged as an important civil rights issue.

The commission has published three volumes that explore the

issue of equal pay for work of "comparative value," focusing on its use as a remedy for sex discrimination in employment. We have already made two recommendations to the President and Congress.

We feel that federal civil rights enforcement agencies, including the Equal Employment Opportunity Commission, should reject comparable worth and rely instead on the principle of equal pay for equal work. Moreover, we recommend that the Justice Department resist comparable worth doctrine in appropriate litigation.

The commission also feels that Congress should not adopt legislation that would establish a comparable worth doctrine in the setting of wages in the federal or private sector.

It is equality of opportunity that allows one to advance toward that laudable goal of a color-blind, race and gender neutral society. Only equality of opportunity will facilitate each individual or group to achieve to the limit of their creativity, imagination and enthusiasm.

Congress and the courts should make a commitment to pursue the moral and constitutional high ground and reject any notion that discrimination can be eliminated or minimized by racial balancing in the form of proportional representation. Nor should Congress condone equality of results in the form of preferential treatment such as quotas, goals, timetables or set-asides.

The main objective of the federal, state and local government must be to provide equal opportunity based upon individual merit. Each of us has an obligation to make sure that our children can compete based upon merit. This means they must be prepared.

A quality education must be available to all children. This nation cannot afford another generation of illiterates of any color.

Derrick Bell, dean of the University of Oregon Law School and a leading force in early court cases to end segregation, has concluded that while "there is potential strength in the argument that school desegregation is needed to improve society, the danger is that this societal personification of the benefit reduces the priority for correction of the harm suffered directly by blacks to a secondary importance when it should be the primary concern."

As W.E.B. DuBois said years ago, "The black child needs neither segregated schools nor mixed schools. What he needs is an education."

I myself survived and prospered without the so-called benefits of affirmative action and integration. The reason for my survival and success is preparation. I attended the all-black Dunbar High School in Washington, D.C. and was given a special gift.

Those black teachers demanded excellence and I left prepared to go forward. I obtained both post secondary degrees from a black college, Howard University, which gave me the tools necessary to achieve success.

We must encourage black people to support black institutions: the black church, black colleges, banks, fraternities, service organizations and countless others. We cannot depend upon philanthropy and charity to save our institutions.

We must create innovative and effective public policy that opens doors and keeps them open. We should be advocating the relaxation and repeal of various regulations that restrict entry and access to the marketplace.

Not only black Americans would benefit from such advocacy. Is it necessary for a barber or beautician to know the name of every bone in the hand to adequately cut hair? Why should a New York City taxi medallion cost $85,000 when a license in Washington, D.C. is only $200? Licensing only serves to restrict access to the market. How many people have $85,000?

Minimum wage also restricts entry into the market by black teenagers. Even the black mayors in the United States believe this to be true, yet many of us continue to work against initiation of legislation to reduce minimum wage.

Finally, affirmative action must be re-evaluated. A program which began with the best intentions and highest ideals has ended up setting white against black. It has created new protected classes, made victim status desirable and forced society to question the accomplishments of its children.

Most tragically, it has created a generation which sees no need to take risk and will never see its rewards. No quota will make any of us successful. No program of quotas will prevent the last of us from failing. Risk taking should be the engine that propels us to success.

Solving the problem of discrimination with more laws and regulations is not the answer. We have a moral responsibility to remove the barriers that deny people access to equal opportunity. We should get rid of special protections that can place more barriers to opportunity.

A passage in *The Essential Rousseau,* "Discourse on Inequality Among Men," written in 1755, sums up the situation:

"Peoples once accustomed to masters are no longer in condition to do without them. If they try to shake off the yoke, they move still farther away from freedom because they confuse it with an unbridled license that is opposed to it, and their revolutions nearly always deliver them into the hands of seducers who only make their chains heavier than before."

Results

It may be fashionable to insist that affirmative action, and especially quotas for minorities, don't work. But not for the first time, the fashion is wrong. In many kinds of situations these remedies do work, providing job opportunities for qualified (or easily qualifiable) people who otherwise would not have them.

This does not mean we should turn to affirmative action to solve all the problems of America's unemployed and under-employed minorities. Affirmative action provides useful tools, not panaceas. Affirmative action cannot make an illiterate person literate, or teach good work habits, or turn someone with janitor's skills into an engineer. There is no substitute for education, training and apprenticeship.

It is clear that the White House, through the Justice Department, opposes any race-related quotas or goals for hiring or promotion of public workers. Although the Supreme Court last year, in the *Stotts* decision, upheld the seniority rights of a group of white firefighters in Memphis, it has not decided whether a racially based formula for public hiring is illegal and unconstitutional.

The Court has now agreed to review a Michigan ruling that upholds an affirmative action plan calling for layoffs of non-minority teachers who have more experience than some minority teachers, but are being laid off in order for the staff to maintain a racial balance.

The administration is arguing that the Supreme Court's ruling in *Stotts* sets the stage for striking down all preferential quotas in hiring and promoting public workers. Recently, the Justice Department has gone to court in a number of cities to overturn hiring agreements that contain racial quotas.

In many circumstances, members of minority groups have been discriminated against casually, thoughtlessly—because it has been the fashion not to hire them. Thus, many big city police and fire departments traditionally hired no blacks; many craft unions accepted no blacks as members; many big companies put no blacks in positions higher than kitchen help and janitors. When patterns of discrimination are apparent, affirmative action and quotas may be valid tools to respond. And they may also be useful for an employer who recognizes the problem and wants to change it voluntarily.

The utility of affirmative action and quotas was demonstrated in 1983 in hearings held by Reps. Don Edwards (D–Cal.) and Patricia Schroeder (D–Colo.). In those hearings I talked about public sector employment in Alabama, something I learned about as an attorney in the Justice Department's civil rights division in the Nixon-Ford administration. Another witness at the same hearings was Fred Cook, vice president for human resources at Mountain Bell in Denver.

Alabama has seen dramatic changes in the level and type of black employment in public agencies over the past decade. Most of that change is directly attributable to litigation and specifically to affirmative action and quota decrees entered by Judge Frank Johnson of Montgomery. And it is tough to imagine how blacks would have gotten those state jobs in Alabama without them.

In the late 1960s, the 70–odd Alabama state agencies employed only a handful of blacks above the menial level. At that time the Justice Department sued seven of the larger agencies which together employed over half the state government's work force. Following trial, Judge Johnson found that of the 1,000 clerical employees in these agencies, only one was black. Of over 2,000 workers in semiprofessional and supervisory positions, just 26 were black.

This paucity of black employees was no accident, since the state refused to recruit at black schools and in black media and also maintained segregated cafeteria facilities.

Even more telling, on those occasions when black applicants appeared at the top of employment registers, agencies simply passed over them in favor of low-ranked whites.

To try to remedy these entrenched discriminatory patterns, Judge Johnson enjoined the passing-over of qualified blacks and required the state to attempt to recruit black applicants. He also ordered the hiring of some 62 blacks who had been passed over and who could be identified following a laborious process of records analysis. In short, Frank Johnson in 1970 ordered everything W. Bradford Reynolds, the current assistant attorney general for civil rights, would require of an employer guilty of discrimination.

But nothing substantive changed, despite Alabama's compliance with the specific elements of Judge Johnson's decree. Perhaps the state's attitude was still too grudging, or blacks were still too skeptical, or perhaps other factors were at work. Whatever the explanation, black employment in Alabama agencies remained low.

The one exception to this otherwise gloomy picture lay in the area of temporary employment. There Johnson had simply imposed a ratio—a quota—on temporary hires. The ratio was fixed at 25 percent—approximately the black population percentage in Alabama—and the goal was met. But there was still no improvement in permanent positions.

Then in January 1972, the Alabama NAACP filed suit against the Department of Public Safety—the state troopers. At that time everyone in Public Safety was white—the troopers, the officers and the support personnel. No blacks had ever been employed there. Throughout the '50s and '60s—from the schoolhouse door to the Selma bridge—the troopers had been the most visible instrument defending segregation.

Judge Johnson set an early trial date, then ruled from the bench, finding that Public Safety had engaged in a "blatant and continuous pattern and practice of discrimination." Having learned from his experience with the other Alabama agencies, Johnson immediately imposed a quota: he required the state to hire one black trooper for each new white hired, until blacks reached 25 percent of the trooper force. He also applied the same formula to support personnel.

The state complied, and the results have been little short of astounding. Within weeks, Alabama had hired its first black troopers. Within two years, there were a substantial number of blacks on the force, and the director of Public Safety later testified that they were competent professionals.

Today, 13 years after the entry of Judge Johnson's decree, Alabama has the most thoroughly integrated state police force in the country. Over 20 percent of the troopers and officers—and nearly 25 percent of the support personnel—are black. The day is fast approaching when Public Safety will be freed of hiring constraints. And although 13 years may seem a long time for a court order to remain in effect, the problem was years longer in the making.

When Justice contrasted the initial results on the trooper force with the lack of progress in other Alabama agencies, the department went back into court, asking that hiring ratios be applied to entry-level jobs in the other Alabama agencies. Judge Johnson gave the agencies plenty of time—over two years—to mend their ways.

When little changed, he issued a decision finding statewide discrimination, but he demurred to Justice's plea for quotas. He said that "mandatory hiring quotas must be a last resort," and he declined to order them. But he noted that the denial would be "without prejudice" to Justice's seeking the same relief one year later: "In the event substantial progress has not been made by the 70 state agencies, hiring goals will then be the only alternative."

The message—the threat—could not have been clearer, and the agencies immediately began to come around. In the eight largest departments, which together account for close to 75 percent of all state workers, black employment increased by over half between 1975 and 1983 and now stands at over 20 percent. And black workers, who used to be concentrated in menial jobs, now appear in substantial numbers in nearly all the larger job categories.

No doubt problems remain in Alabama, but the only fair conclusion is that dramatic progress has been achieved in public employment for blacks over the past decade. And in view of the history of the Alabama litigation, it is clear that this would not have occurred if Judge Johnson had not first imposed a hiring quota on the state troopers—and then threatened to extend it statewide if the other agencies did not alter their discriminatory practices.

At Mountain Bell—an affiliate of AT&T before divestiture—affirmative action was also needed. In 1972, AT&T entered into a six-year consent decree with the EEOC and the Justice Department to substantially increase the number of minority and female workers, as well as the number of women in non-traditional jobs such as installers, cable repairers and frame attendants.

It was not easy at first. Fred Cook said Mountain Bell did not meet its goals for the first year of the decree, but the company then intensified its recruiting efforts and was on target for the next five. As a result, minority managers at the company have increased from under 200 to over 1,400, and there are now nearly 1,200 women in non-traditional jobs, compared to 81 in the year before the decree.

Cook defends Mountain Bell's employment practices in the '50s and '60s, saying that his company was more responsive than most to the aspirations of minorities and female workers. But, he frankly admits that the consent decree focused the company's efforts in a particularly acute and compelling way. As he put it, "It became as important as the bottom line." If it weren't for the decree, with its affirmative action goals, the progress Cook recounted would not have been made.

It is also significant that affirmative action has helped Mountain Bell in a very practical way. Fred Cook said recently that, before the consent decree, "we were reflecting society. We were not using all the talent available." Under the decree, though, the company discovered that its minority and female work force was a "gold mine" for high-quality managers.

And in the wake of Mountain Bell's own efforts, blacks, Hispanics, and women formed organizations aimed at helping one another and at assisting the company in identifying still more talent. Cook praised the work of these groups, and he said that the net result is that Mountain Bell has done a "very good job, especially since the consent decree has ended." The company has no interest in turning back. According to Cook, "it is good business sense to take this kind of affirmative action." It is ironic that it took government action to sharpen Bell's business judgment.

Affirmative action can be a potent weapon, so it should be used only with great care. An effective affirmative action program should have a limited duration, should be aimed only at genuine problems caused by past discrimination, and should not lower standards. Otherwise the problem of selection based on race or sex may be perpetuated indefinitely.

In deciding whether affirmative action is desirable or required, the key question is, what caused a company to exclude blacks from its work force, or keep them in menial jobs? When the answer is that blacks did not have the requisite skills or training, then affirmative action is unlikely to be an effective remedy.

But when the cause is discrimination, whether it is overt or casual discrimination, affirmative action may then be required.

MAJOR U.S. SUPREME COURT DECISIONS, JANUARY–JUNE 1989[2]

Of all the civil rights issues with which the U.S. Supreme Court has grappled in recent years, none has been as divisive as

[2]Excerpts from an article by Samuel Rabinove, legal director, American Jewish Committee. Prepared June 30, 1989. Reprinted with permission.

that of affirmative action, which is clearly a matter of rights in conflict. Hence, it is not surprising that the Court has often failed to send clear signals to the country as to the proper limits of affirmative action remedies in employment discrimination cases. For example, in the leading case of *Griggs v. Duke Power Company* in 1971, the Court ruled unanimously that "discriminatory preference for any group, minority or majority, is precisely and only what Congress has proscribed in Title VII" of the Civil Rights Act of 1964. (The Court in *Griggs* ruled also that job qualification standards must be job performance related, and it placed on employers the burden of proving, as an affirmative defense, that practices that are shown to have a discriminatory or disparate impact on racial minorities are actually justified by business necessity.) In *Furnco Construction Corp. v. Waters* in 1978, the Court (7–2) said: "It is clear beyond cavil that the obligation imposed by Title VII is to provide an equal opportunity to *each* applicant regardless of race without regard to whether members of the applicant's race are already proportionately represented in the work force."

Yet, just one year later, in *United Steel Workers v. Weber,* the Court ruled (5–2) that it is not unlawful under Title VII for a private employer (Kaiser Aluminum & Chemical Company in Louisiana) voluntarily to establish quotas or preferences for black workers to eliminate racial imbalance in traditionally white-only job categories, provided these do not "unnecessarily trammel" the interests of white employees. And, in 1980 in *Fullilove v. Klutznick,* the Court upheld (5–3) a 10% minority set-aside in a Federal public works law enacted by Congress. On the other hand, in *Firefighters Local Union #1784 v. Stotts* in 1984, the Court held (6–3) that Title VII bars a court from ordering an employer to lay off employees with greater seniority in favor of those with lesser seniority, in order to preserve a certain percentage of blacks in the work force.

In 1986, in *Local 28, Sheet Metal Workers v. Equal Employment Opportunity Commission,* where there was egregious union discrimination for many years, coupled with defiance of numerous injunctions to cease discriminating, the Court approved (5–4) a lower court order that imposed on the union a race conscious numerical remedy, a goal of 29 percent black and Hispanic membership. The following year, in *United States v. Paradise,* the Court also upheld (5–4) a promotion quota imposed by a lower court after a finding of persistent discrimination against blacks by the state of Alabama in hiring and promoting highway patrol officers, requiring the state to promote one black trooper for each white from a pool of qualified candidates, even if the whites scored higher on tests. Also in 1987, in *Johnson v. Transportation Agency, Santa Clara County, California*, the Court rejected (6–3) a challenge by a white male to a voluntary affirmative-action plan, implemented by a public agency to redress underrepresentation of women and minorities in skilled job classifications, which gave a job as road dispatcher to a white woman who had scored slightly less than the man on an oral examination.

These are but a few of many possible illustrations of how the Supreme Court has been divided in affirmative action cases, depending on the facts of the cases and the perceptions at the time of the Justices who heard them. It should be stressed that these were all complicated cases, their facts differed widely, and the law is by no means crystal clear. Further, the Justices have always been sharply split and at least some of them have been deeply ambivalent about the wisdom and proper scope of preferential remedies based on race or sex that were designed to cure historic discrimination.

City of Richmond v. J.A. Croson Co.

In its ruling on January 23, 1989 in this case, the U.S. Supreme Court struck down a Richmond law that channeled 30% of public works funds to minority-owned construction companies. In so doing, however, the Court raised serious constitutional questions about a wide variety of governmental contract and hiring programs designed to aid racial minorities.

In six separate opinions the Court ruled (6–3) that the Richmond ordinance, similar to minority set-aside programs in 36 states and nearly 200 local governments, violated the constitutional rights of white contractors to equal protection of the law under the Fourteenth Amendment. The opinion of the Court, written by Justice Sandra Day O'Connor, said that such programs could be justified only if they served the "compelling state interest" of redressing "identified discrimination," whether by the government itself or by private parties. "Societal" discrimination alone will not suffice. Key portions of her opinion were joined by Chief Justice William H. Rehnquist and Justices Byron R. White, Anthony M. Kennedy and John Paul Stevens. Justice Antonin Scalia provided a sixth vote for the result in a separate opinion.

Justice O'Connor said that any "rigid numerical quota," no matter how small, is suspect. She said also that the statistical disparities in Richmond fell far short of proving that specific acts of discrimination had occurred. In her words, "an amorphous claim that there has been past discrimination in a particular industry cannot justify the use of an unyielding racial quota." Yet, in the five years before the set-aside ordinance took effect, fewer than 1% of Richmond's construction contracts went to black companies. After that, it rose to the mandated 30%. Then, in 1987 when a lower court invalidated the set-aside, contracts awarded to blacks fell to 2%.

In distinguishing the Court's decision in the earlier case of *Fullilove v. Klutznick,* Justice O'Connor noted that actions by Congress to redress racial discrimination rest on a solid constitutional base that is not available to states and localities. Section 5 of the Fourteenth Amendment gave Congress alone broad discretion to decide what the country needed to promote racial equality.

Justice O'Connor found not a shred of evidence of past discrimination against Spanish-speaking, Oriental, Indian, Eskimo or Aleut persons in any part of Richmond's construction industry. Hence, she wrote, the plan's random inclusion of those groups strongly impugns the city's claim of remedial motivation. Moreover, in her view, the plan was not narrowly tailored to remedy the effects of prior discrimination, since it entitled racial minority entrepreneurs from anywhere in the country to an absolute preference over other citizens, based solely on their race.

Justice O'Connor concluded that if the city could identify past discrimination in the local construction industry with the particularity required by the Equal Protection Clause, it would have the power to adopt race-based legislation designed to eradicate the effects of that discrimination. She said also: "The relevant statistical pool for purposes of demonstrating discriminatory exclusion must be the number of minorities qualified to undertake the particular task." In the light of this rationale, the most pressing question would seem to be the nature and content of the evidence a local government would have to amass in order to meet the Court's stringent criteria.

Justice Thurgood Marshall, joined by Justices William J. Brennan, Jr. and Harry A. Blackmun, wrote a scathing dissent. In his words:

Cynical of one municipality's attempt to redress the effects of past racial discrimination in a particular industry, the majority launches a grapeshot attack on race-conscious remedies in general. The majority's unnecessary pronouncements will inevitably discourage or prevent governmental entities, particularly States and localities, from acting to rectify the scourge of past discrimination. This is the harsh reality of the majority's decision, but it is not the Constitution's command.

Although there is language in the majority opinions that understandably is disquieting to supporters of far-reaching affirmative action, the Supreme Court certainly did not invalidate all government-sponsored affirmative action programs. Nor did the Justices even necessarily bar the particular kind of affirmative action that was directly at issue in this case, i.e., minority set-asides. What the Court did say was that all racial classifications are equally suspect and will be subjected to "strict scrutiny." This means that any law that gives members of one race a preference must be shown to have been tailored as narrowly as possible to meet the "compelling state interest" of curing identified discrimination in order to survive a constitutional challenge. The problem, however, is that the thrust of the decision, and at least some of the language of the majority opinions, may well have a deterrent effect on affirmative action programs in general.

Price Waterhouse v. Hopkins

On May 1, the Supreme Court ruled (6–3) in a technical and rather complicated case of alleged intentional discrimination, that an employer has the burden of proving that its refusal to hire or promote a person is based on non-discriminatory grounds. Price Waterhouse claimed that a woman employee who was refused a partnership in the accounting firm had the burden of proving that it was sex discrimination that cost her that position, rather than legitimate judgments as to her capabilities. The high Court, in an opinion by Justice Brennan, rejected the firm's argument. The Court said also that evidence that Ms. Hopkins was evaluated by her male supervisors on the basis of stereotyped views of appropriate female appearance and behavior (one partner described her as "macho," another advised her to take "a course at charm school," several criticized her use of profanity) can establish the existence of unlawful sex discrimination.

Although the District of Columbia Circuit Court of Appeals had ruled that Price Waterhouse was required to submit "clear and convincing" proof that its reasons for denying Ms. Hopkins a partnership were non-discriminatory, the Supreme Court did make it easier on the firm in one respect by ruling that it could be held only to the lesser standard of "a preponderance of the evidence" to support its claim that it had legitimate reasons to deny her a partnership. The case was remanded to the lower court for reconsideration under the less rigorous standard.

It should be stressed that this case involves an allegation of intentional discrimination, or disparate treatment, rather than discriminatory or disparate impact without intent to discriminate. The nature of the case is important because it relates to the critical question of which side must carry the burden of proof. In this case there was evidence that the employer's denial of a partnership to the woman plaintiff may have been based on reasons some of which may have been legitimate and others that may have been discriminatory. In such a "mixed motive" case, the burden of oof may be almost insurmountable to a plaintiff who may have ome evidence of discrimination, but who lacks sufficient information to meet the burden of showing that discrimination was the crucial factor. Hence, the Court's ruling that an employer has the burden of proving that its refusal to promote was based on legitimate rather than discriminatory reasons is significant. In sum, the Court made it somewhat easier for a plaintiff to prevail in a case charging intentional discrimination or disparate treatment in employment for reasons of sex, race or age.

There was no single majority opinion in the case. Justice Brennan's opinion, announcing the judgment of the Court, was joined by Justices Marshall, Blackmun and Stevens. Justice O'Connor wrote a separate concurring opinion, as did Justice White. The chief difference between these concurring opinions and that of Justice Brennan was that these Justices would require a plaintiff to show initially that discrimination was at least a "substantial" factor in the company's decision adverse to the plaintiff, with the company then having to prove that the adverse decision would have been made anyway. In contrast, Justice Brennan's opinion requires the plaintiff to show initially only that discrimination was a "motivating" factor in the adverse decision.

Justice Kennedy dissented, in an opinion joined by Chief Justice Rehnquist and Justice Scalia. In their view, the plaintiff had failed to meet the requisite standard of proof of discrimination. The dissenters contended also that the Court's approach to the complex rules for judging employment discrimination cases is "certain to result in confusion." Said Justice Kennedy: "The ultimate question in every individual disparate treatment case is

whether discrimination caused the particular decision at issue . . . That decision was for the finder of fact, however, and the
District Court made plain that sex discrimination was not a but-
for cause of the decision to place Hopkins' partnership candidacy
on hold . . . Hopkins thus failed to meet the requisite standard of
proof after a full trial."

Wards Cove Packing Company, Inc. v. Atonio

Do employers who are sued under Title VII of the Civil Rights
Act of 1964 have the burden of justifying, on grounds of "business necessity," practices that are shown to have a discriminatory
impact on minorities or women? On June 5, the U.S. Supreme
Court said "no" (5–4). The Court ruled that when a Title VII
plaintiff uses statistics to establish a prima facie case of unlawful
discrimination, the employer must provide evidence only of a
legitimate reason for the challenged practice. Further, the burden
of proving that such a practice is not a form of unlawful discrimination does not shift to the employer, the Court said. Justice
White, who delivered the opinion of the Court, declared that the
plaintiff "bears the burden of disproving an employer's assertion
that the adverse employment action or practice was based solely
on a legitimate neutral consideration."

The decision also limited the type of statistical evidence that
minorities can use to prove discrimination. In this regard, Justice
White said that a lack of minority group members in skilled jobs is
not valid evidence if that statistic merely reflects "a dearth of
qualified non-white applicants for reasons that are not an employer's fault."

The case arose when non-white cannery workers at the company's Alaskan salmon canneries charged that the company's hiring and promotion practices were responsible for racial stratifica-
tion in the work force. Eskimo and Filipino workers on the
factory lines allegedly were denied access to the better-paid skilled
jobs, which were filled predominantly by white workers. The
Court ruled that a comparison of the percentage of cannery
workers who were non-white with the percentage of non-cannery
workers who were non-white does not in itself establish a prima
facie "disparate impact" case. Rather, said the Court, the proper
comparison is between racial composition of the jobs in question
and the racial composition of the qualified population in the relevant labor market. A mere showing that non-whites are under-

represented in the skilled jobs will not suffice. The Court said that the courts below must require proof that the statistical disparity complained of is the result of employment practices that are being attacked, specifically showing that each challenged practice has a significantly "disparate impact" on employment opportunities for non-whites.

Justice White said that the plaintiffs must show not only that specific policies created the disparities, but that the employer had no legitimate business justification for the practices in question. In his view, this "burden of persuasion" fell naturally on Title VII plaintiffs, rather than on the employer, because it is the plaintiffs who must prove that they were discriminated against. The Court remanded the case to the lower courts with instructions to permit the plaintiffs to show, on some other basis, that the under-representation of minority groups in the skilled jobs violated Title VII. In sum, the Court made it significantly easier for employers to defend hiring and promotion practices that may have a discriminatory impact on members of racial minorities and women.

Chief Justice Rehnquist and Justices O'Connor, Scalia and Kennedy joined in Justice White's opinion. Justice Stevens filed a dissenting opinion, as did Justice Blackmun. Justices Brennan and Marshall joined both dissenting opinions. The dissenters accused the Court of rejecting its own previous rulings in Title VII cases (*Griggs v. Duke Power Company,* in particular) and of turning its back on the nation's long history of racial discrimination. In the words of Justice Blackmun's brief dissent: "One wonders whether the majority still believes that race discrimination—or, more accurately, race discrimination against non-whites—is a problem in our society, or even remembers that it ever was." In Justice Steven's lengthy dissent, he said:

Fully eighteen years ago, this Court unanimously held that Title VII of the Civil Rights Act of 1964 prohibits employment practices that have discriminatory effects as well as those that are intended to discriminate. *Griggs v. Duke Power Company* . . . Decisions of this Court and other Federal courts repeatedly have recognized that while the employer's burden in a disparate treatment case is simply one of coming forward with evidence of legitimate business purpose, its burden in a disparate impact case is proof of an affirmative defense of business necessity.

Although this decision does not explicitly overrule the Court's decision in *Griggs,* implicitly, at least, it comes very close to having done so, and thus represents a measurable setback to the cause of equal employment opportunity for racial minorities and women.

Martin v. Wilks

The key question in this case was whether or not white men, who were not involved in litigation leading to a court-approved affirmative action plan which gave preferences to minorities or women, can subsequently challenge such a plan as a violation of Title VII? On June 12, the Supreme Court said (5–4) that they can do so, that such suits may be filed even years after the affirmative action plan took effect. Interpreting the Federal Rules of Civil Procedure, Chief Justice Rehnquist wrote for the Court: "A voluntary settlement in the form of a consent decree between one group of employees and their employer cannot possibly settle, voluntarily or otherwise, the conflicting claims of another group of employees who do not join in the agreement."

This decision permits white firefighters in Birmingham, Alabama, to attack an eight-year old, court-approved settlement which was intended to increase the numbers of blacks hired and promoted by the fire department. It means that consent decrees that have settled so many racial discrimination suits, which have long been regarded as immune to subsequent legal challenge by outside parties, may now be only the opening round in a new phase of litigation. The Court thus rejected a doctrine known as "impermissible collateral attack," which would protect parties to a consent decree from discrimination charges by others based on actions mandated by the decree. The ruling also applies, of course, to decrees that resolved sex discrimination cases. The Court did not indicate whether any time limits would be placed on such subsequent actions, which Chief Justice Rehnquist characterized as "reverse discrimination" suits.

In his opinion, which was joined by Justices White, O'Connor, Scalia and Kennedy, the Chief Justice acknowledged the prevailing judicial view that if individuals choose not to intervene in a suit that might ultimately affect them, "they should not be permitted to later litigate the issues in a new action." The Chief Justice said: "The position has sufficient appeal to have commanded the approval of the great majority of the Federal Courts of Appeals, but we agree with the contrary view expressed by the Court of Appeals for the Eleventh Circuit in this case." In the majority's view, the Chief Justice declared: "A judgment or decree among parties to a law suit resolves issues as among them, but it does not conclude the rights of strangers to those proceedings." Based on this language, it appears that the decision opens up to subsequent dispute not merely court-approved settlements but also judgments resulting from full trials.

The Birmingham firefighters' case began in the early 1970s when the local chapter of the NAACP, supported by the Government, sued the city on the ground that blacks were being discriminated against in hiring and promotion by the fire department. After several years of litigation, a settlement was reached. But the union that represented the department's almost completely white work force objected to the settlement. The U.S. District Court approved it nonetheless and entered a consent decree under which blacks and whites would be hired and promoted in equal numbers until the number of black firefighters approximated the proportion of blacks in the civilian labor force. Several months later a group of white firefighters sued the city, arguing that the consent decree discriminated against them. The District Court dismissed this suit on the ground that the city could not be guilty of discrimination if it was complying with the mandate of a consent decree. In 1987, the Eleventh Circuit Court of Appeals overturned the District Court's dismissal and reinstated the white firefighters' discrimination suit. The city, along with a group of black firefighters, then appealed to the Supreme Court.

Justice Stevens filed a dissenting opinion, warning that the decision would serve to discourage voluntary settlements of discrimination complaints, in which Justices Brennan, Marshall and Blackmun joined. Justice Stevens said also:

In a case such as this . . . in which there has been no showing that the decree was collusive, fraudulent, transparently invalid, or entered without jurisdiction, it would be 'unconscionable' to conclude that obedience to an order remedying a Title VII violation could subject a defendant to an additional liability . . . would subject large employers who seek to comply with the law remedying past discrimination to a never-ending stream of litigation and potential liability. It is unfathomable that either Title VII or the Equal Protection Clause demands such a counter-productive result.

This decision is most unsettling. By enabling interested parties, e.g., white males, to reopen discrimination cases long believed to have been closed it may have the effect of unraveling significant gains in employment by racial minorities and women that had been thought secure.

Lorance v. AT&T Technologies, Inc.

What is the background of this case? Before 1979, collective-bargaining agreements between AT&T Technologies, Inc. and

Local 1942, International Brotherhood of Electrical Workers, AFL-CIO, had determined a worker's seniority on the basis of years of *plantwide* service, and plantwide seniority was transferable upon promotion to a more skilled "tester" position. A new agreement executed in 1979 changed this by making seniority in *tester* jobs dependent upon the amount of time spent as a *tester*. In 1982 three women employees, who were promoted to tester positions between 1978 and 1980, received demotions during an economic downturn that they would not have experienced had the former seniority system remained in place. They filed charges with the Equal Employment Opportunity Commission in 1983 and, after receiving right-to-sue letters, filed an action in U.S. District Court. They alleged that their rights had been violated under Title VII of the Civil Rights Act of 1964 by adoption of the new seniority system with the purpose and effect of protecting incumbent testers—jobs traditionally dominated by men—from female employees who had greater plantwide seniority and who were becoming testers in increasing numbers. The court rejected their claims on the ground that they had not been filed within the required period "after the alleged unfair labor practice occurred." The Seventh Circuit Court of Appeals affirmed that ruling.

On June 12, the U.S. Supreme Court affirmed (5–3) the judgment of the Court of Appeals, thereby imposing stringent time limitations on the filing of law suits challenging seniority systems that are alleged to be discriminatory. In an opinion by Justice Scalia, joined by Chief Justice Rehnquist and Justices White, Stevens, and Kennedy, the Court ruled that such challenges must be brought within 300 days of the *adoption* of the seniority system that is alleged to be discriminatory. (Title VII suits must be filed within 300 days of the alleged discrimination.) In other words, they were too late.

In the opinion for the majority, Justice Scalia said that the Court's precedents concerning discriminatory seniority systems made it clear that it is the adoption of the system, and not its consequences, that is the "discriminatory act" under Title VII. In his words: "Allowing a facially neutral system to be challenged, and entitlements under it to be altered, many years after its adoption would disrupt" the legitimate interests of other employees who benefitted from the changes.

In a dissenting opinion, joined by Justices Brennan and Blackmun, Justice Marshall said that "nothing in the text of Title VII compels this result." He went on to say:

The majority today continues the process of immunizing seniority systems from the requirements of Title VII. In addition to the other hurdles previously put in place by the Court, employees must now anticipate, and initiate suit to prevent, future adverse applications of a seniority system, no matter how speculative or unlikely these applications may be.

In the view of the dissenting Justices, Congress in enacting Title VII never intended to confer "absolute immunity on discriminatorily adopted seniority systems that survive their first 300 days." They accused the majority of a "severe interpretation" of the law, which in effect is not fair to an employee who subsequently challenges a system that at the time of its *adoption*, the employee could not reasonably have expected to be detrimental to her or him.

Patterson v. McLean Credit Union

Last year, in an unusual action in this case, the U.S. Supreme Court decided to reconsider the rights of minorities to sue private parties for racial discrimination under the old Civil Rights Act of 1866. Five Justices, over strenuous dissents by the other four, agreed to consider overruling the Court's major decision in 1976 in the case of *Runyon v. McCrary* that had expanded such rights. The Court took this action on its own initiative; the parties to *Patterson v. McLean Credit Union* had not sought it. The Court's action sent shock waves through the civil rights community. (AJC joined in an *amicus* brief with many other civil rights groups urging the Court not to overrule *Runyon*.)

The majority ordered the lawyers in *Patterson*, a case the Court had already heard, to present new arguments on whether to overturn the earlier ruling. The question was whether the Court had erred in its ruling in *Runyon* (7–2) that the law to guarantee the rights of the newly freed slaves, passed by Congress soon after the Civil War, was intended to bar racial discrimination by private schools, employers and other parties in deciding with whom they will contract or do business. The statute provides, in pertinent part, that all persons shall have the same right "to make and enforce contracts . . . as is enjoyed by white citizens." It is now codified in the United States Code as 42 U.S.C. §1981.

Until the 1960s, this law was used to attack state and local laws that interfered with the business and contractual rights of minorities. But in the 1960s and 1970s, civil rights lawyers began using it successfully to attack as well private discrimination (including employment discrimination on the job). That led to *Runyon*.

The immediate ruling in *Runyon* was that black people could sue private schools for denying them admission on racial grounds. But its broad reasoning also applied generally to racial discrimination in private transactions. One major effect was to give victims of job discrimination broader protections and more potent remedies, e.g., the ability to sue for punitive damages, than are provided by the Civil Rights Act of 1964. In *Patterson,* the Court originally agreed simply to consider the question of whether a black woman teller at a North Carolina credit union, who said she was harassed and discriminated against by her employer on account of her race, could sue her employer for damages under §1981.

On June 15, the Supreme Court unanimously decided against overruling *Runyon.* Simultaneously, however, the high Court ruled (5–4) that §1981 cannot serve as the basis for a law suit alleging racial harassment in the work place. Justice Kennedy, writing for the Court, said that while §1981 did prohibit discrimination at the initial hiring stage, it did not prohibit discriminatory treatment on the job. In the majority's view, Congress never intended that the Civil Rights Act of 1866 should go any further. Justice Kennedy said:

But the right to make contracts does not extend, as a matter of either logic or semantics, to conduct by the employer after the contract relation has been established, including breach of the terms of the contract or imposition of discriminatory working conditions.

Having held as it did, Justice Kennedy's opinion nonetheless declared: "The law now reflects society's consensus that discrimination based on the color of one's skin is a profound wrong of tragic dimension." He said, moreover, that neither the Court's words nor its decisions "should be interpreted as signaling one inch of retreat from Congress's policy to forbid discrimination in the private, as well as the public sphere." Justice Kennedy's opinion was joined by Chief Justice Rehnquist and Justices White, O'Connor and Scalia (the same five Justices who had ordered reargument of the case last year.)

Justice Brennan, joined in his rather heated dissent by Justices Marshall, Blackmun and Stevens (in part), began his opinion by charging: "What the Court declines to snatch away with one hand, it takes with the other." He went on to accuse the majority of giving "this landmark, civil rights statute a needlessly cramped interpretation." Moreover, said Justice Brennan:

When it comes to deciding whether a civil rights statute should be construed to further our Nation's commitment to the eradication of racial discrimination, the Court adopts a formalistic method of interpretation antithetical to Congress' vision of a society in which contractual opportunities are equal.

After observing: "Some members of this Court believe that *Runyon* was decided incorrectly," Justice Kennedy said that there was no need for the Court to decide in this case whether the *Runyon* decision was either right or wrong, because it is not "inconsistent with the prevailing sense of justice in this country." Justice Brennan, however, insisted that the *Runyon* decision was correct at the time it was decided.

Justice Kennedy did not say what had motivated the Court to order reargument in this case. He did list reasons why the Court had previously overturned precedents and then indicated why these did not apply to the *Runyon* decision. He said that the "primary reason" for the Court to overrule precedents interpreting Federal statutes was an "intervening development," either in judicial doctrine or through an act of Congress, that has "removed or weakened the conceptual underpinnings from the prior decision." But this had not happened with respect to *Runyon*, he said. Nor was *Runyon* either "unworkable or confusing." He was careful to distinguish, however, between cases interpreting Federal law and those interpreting constitutional provisions, noting that the Court has traditionally been more reluctant to overturn Federal statutory interpretations for the reason that Congress is free to do so itself if the Court has misinterpreted a Congressional action. By contrast, since the Court is the ultimate interpreter of the Constitution, only the Court itself, absent a constitutional amendment, can correct an interpretation it later comes to view as erroneous.

Whatever one's view may be as to the correct interpretation of §1981, there can be little doubt that the Court's restrictive interpretation severely weakens it as a weapon against discrimination in employment.

Jett v. Dallas Independent School District

This case concerns the interpretation of the same statute that was at issue in *Patterson v. McLean Credit Union.* On June 22, the U.S. Supreme Court ruled (5–4) that the Civil Rights Act of 1866, §1981, cannot be used to bring damage suits against state or local governments for acts of racial discrimination. In an opinion by Justice O'Connor, containing a lengthy exposition of the legislative histories of the civil rights laws of 1866 and 1871, the Court ruled that Congress had intended the later civil rights act of 1871, now codified as §1983, to provide the exclusive remedy for bringing such damage suits. Section 1983 gives individuals the right to challenge official actions that allegedly deprive them of constitutional or Federal statutory rights. In the words of Justice O'Connor:

We think the history of the 1866 Act and the 1871 Act recounted above indicates that Congress intended that the explicit remedial provisions of §1983 be controlling in the context of damages actions brought against state actors alleging violation of the rights declared in §1981.

The significance of this ruling is that it makes it more difficult for a plaintiff to prevail in such a suit because the plaintiff must prove that the discrimination in question was not a random act of an individual public employee, but rather resulted from an official "policy or custom." Since most governmental entities today have official policies *against* racial discrimination, it will not be easy for plaintiffs to sustain this burden of proof.

Justice O'Connor's opinion was joined by Chief Justice Rehnquist and Justices White, Scalia (in most respects) and Kennedy, the same five who interpreted §1981 narrowly in *Patterson v. McLean Credit Union*. Justices Marshall, Blackmun and Stevens joined in a dissenting opinion filed by Justice Brennan. Justice Brennan, after lamenting that the underlying issue of whether §1981 could be used at all in suits against governmental agencies was brought to the Court belatedly and was not fully briefed, declared:

Because I would conclude that §1981 itself affords a cause of action in damages on the basis of governmental conduct violating its terms, and because I would conclude that such an action may be predicated on a theory of *respondeat superior*, I dissent . . . During the period when . . . the 1866 Act was enacted, and for over 100 years thereafter, the federal courts routinely concluded that a statute setting forth substantive rights without specifying a remedy contained an implied cause of action for damages incurred in violation of the statute's terms.

Until this ruling, lower Federal courts had interpreted §1981 to permit damage suits against state and local governments. Under these decisions, governmental bodies were held responsible for discriminatory acts of their employees under a theory of "vicarious liability," without any need to show that the employee was carrying out an official policy. Consequently, §1981, which guarantees to blacks the same right "to make and enforce contracts" and to the same "full and equal benefit of all laws" as whites, was frequently invoked by civil rights plaintiffs when suing government agencies.

The case arose when a white high school football coach, Norman Jett, employed by the Dallas Independent School District, was fired by a black principal, resulting in a lawsuit charging racial discrimination. He won a $650,000 award against the school district on the basis that the district was liable for the action of the principal. The Fifth Circuit Court of Appeals, however, reversed this decision. It ruled that the "vicarious liability" interpretation of §1981 was wrong and that the official "policy or custom" approach of §1983 should apply. In the plaintiff's appeal to the Supreme Court, the high Court majority affirmed in part the Fifth Circuit's decision, and then went beyond it to hold that §1983 was the only law under which such a suit for damages can be brought. While the Civil Rights Act of 1964, which broadly bars discrimination in employment, can also be used to sue government employers, it permits plaintiffs to sue only for back pay and not for other types of damages.

What Does It All Mean?

What comes through with great force from these recent civil rights decisions is this: where the language of a law and/or its legislative history is not that clear, where judicial precedents provided by earlier cases are not definitive, where the issue is one of two rights in conflict both of which make a plausible claim for a favorable ruling in terms of justice, the Supreme Court Justices are likely to vote in accord with their underlying political and social philosophies. In this regard, the so-called "conservative-liberal" split in this Court is nothing new—historically, it was ever thus. Only the issues are different.

There can be no serious question that on civil rights issues, at least, the Supreme Court pendulum has swung to the "right." There is now in place a solid "conservative" majority of five. Its recent watershed decisions, taken together, are likely to make discrimination suits more difficult to bring, more difficult to win, and more vulnerable to challenge if, in fact, they are won. They will assuredly have a chilling effect on the aspirations of racial minorities and women.

The chief reason for this shift to the "right" is the new complexion of the bench resulting from former President Reagan's three appointments. In 1981, Justice O'Connor was appointed to replace retiring Justice Stewart. While Justice Stewart was considered to be moderately conservative, on balance he was less "conservative" than Justice O'Connor has recently proved to be on civil rights issues. Justice Stewart, for example, voted with the majority in 1979 in the major pro-affirmative action decision in *United Steel Workers v. Weber.*

More recently, Justice Scalia, who took the seat vacated by Justice Rehnquist upon the accession of the latter to the post of Chief Justice when former Chief Justice Burger retired, has proved to be more "conservative" on civil rights issues than the Justice he replaced. Former Chief Justice Burger, for example, while certainly no "flaming liberal," wrote the pro-affirmative action majority opinion in *Fullilove v. Klutznick* in 1980 (noted in the Introduction to this paper). Justice Scalia, as has Justice O'Connor, has voted on the same side as staunchly "conservative" Chief Justice Rehnquist in approximately 80% of the cases before the Court.

Justice Kennedy, who replaced retiring Justice Powell, based on his recent opinions, is clearly more "conservative" than was his predecessor. Justice Powell tended to adopt a middle ground position with regard to affirmative action remedies. In the 1978 case of *University of California Regents v. Bakke,* for example, although he rejected the quota remedy, stressing that the Equal Protection Clause guaranteed protection to all individuals regardless of race, he held also that race and ethnicity may be taken into account in the admissions process of the state university since racial and ethnic diversity is a valid educational objective. And, in the case of *Local 28, Sheet Metal Workers v. Equal Employment Opportunity Commission* (noted in the Introduction), Justice Powell, once again (as he did in *Bakke*) providing the crucial fifth vote to make a majority, said that "the imposition of flexible goals as a remedy for past discrimination may be permissible under the Constitution."

Finally, Justice White, who has served on the bench for 27 years, quite simply has changed his mind on civil rights issues. While he, too, was part of the pro-affirmative action majority in *United Steel Workers v. Weber,* it seems clear from his recent opinions and votes that he now believes that *Weber* was wrongly decided. Justice White wrote the opinion for the majority in *Firefighters Local Union #1784 v. Stotts* (noted in the Introduction) in 1984, in which the Court refused to allow layoffs of more senior workers in order to preserve affirmative action gains.

Looking ahead to what may be in store during the years to come, each of the three most "liberal" Justices (Brennan, Marshall, Blackmun) is more than 80 years old. As lawyers say, *res ipsa loquitur*—the thing speaks for itself—or so it would appear.

There are presently moves afoot in Congress to undo through legislation at least some of the effects of the Supreme Court's retreat on civil rights. This will not be easy to accomplish. It took four years for Congress to enact the Civil Rights Restoration Act, which effectively overturned the Supreme Court's limiting decision in *Grove City College v. Bell,* by applying Federal anti-discrimination laws to entire institutions that accept Federal funds, rather than only to the specific programs in such institutions that are helped by such funds. And, very importantly, as of this writing, President Bush has said that "my advice from the Attorney General is that legislation isn't necessary."

The Court's ruling in *City of Richmond v. Croson,* since it was based on constitutional grounds, is not susceptible to statutory correction. An attempt to overturn the decision in *Wards Cove Packing Co. v. Atonio* would surely trigger intense debate because it would require altering the structure of Title VII. And the Court's ruling in *Martin v. Wilks* was based not on a particular statute but rather on an interpretation of the procedural rules that govern the Federal courts. With regard to *Jett v. Dallas Independent School District,* state and local government almost certainly would resist Congressional moves to tamper with the decision which, for them, is wonderful. In any event, efforts will surely be made to limit through some legislation, to the maximum extent possible, the impact of the Court's recent rulings. Perhaps the least difficult one to correct is *Patterson v. McLean Credit Union* because of a probable broad political consensus in support of expanding the scope of §1981. It remains to be seen how successful these various efforts will be.

THE SUPREME COURT AND CIVIL RIGHTS: HAS THE TIDE TURNED?[3]

For many years, no institution of American government has been as close a friend to civil rights as the United States Supreme Court. Make no mistake, I do not mean for a moment to denigrate the considerable contributions to the enhancement of civil rights by presidents, the Congress, other Federal courts, and the legislatures and judiciaries of many states.

However, we must recognize that the Court's approach to civil rights cases has changed markedly. Its recent opinions vividly illustrate this changed judicial attitude. In *Richmond v. Croson*, the Court took a broad swipe at affirmative action, making it extraordinarily hard for any state or city to fashion a race-conscious remedial program that will survive its constitutional scrutiny. Indeed, the Court went so far as to express its doubts that the effects of past racial discrimination still are felt in the city of Richmond, Va., and in society as a whole.

Further, in a series of cases interpreting Federal civil rights statutes—*Price Waterhouse v. Hopkins; Martin v. Wilks; Lorance v. AT&T Technologies, Inc.; Will v. Michigan Department of State Police;* and *Jett v. Dallas Independent School District*—the Court imposed new and stringent procedural requirements that make it more and more difficult for the civil rights plaintiff to gain vindication.

The most striking feature of these opinions was the expansiveness of their holdings, often addressing broad issues, wholly unnecessary to the decisions. To strike down the set-aside plan in *Richmond*, for example, there was no need to decide anything other than that the plan was too imprecisely tailored. Instead, the Court chose to deliver a discourse on the narrow limits within which the states and localities may engage in affirmative action and on the special infirmities of plans passed by cities with minority leaders.

The Court was even more aggressive in revisiting settled statutory issues under Section 1981 and Title VII. In *Patterson v. McLean Credit Union*, it took the extraordinary step of calling for rebriefing on a question that no party had raised—whether the

[3]Reprint of an article by Supreme Court Justice Thurgood Marshall. From USA TODAY MAGAZINE, March copyright 1990 by the Society for the Advancement of Education.

Court, in the 1976 case of *Runyon v. McCrary,* wrongly had held Section 1981 to apply to private acts of racial discrimination. In *Ward's Cove v. Atonio,* the Court implicitly overruled *Griggs v. Duke Power Co.,* another established precedent which had required employers to bear the burden of justifying employment practices with a disparate impact on groups protected by Title VII. Henceforth, the burden will be on the employees to prove that these practices are justified.

Stare decisis [the doctrine that principles of law established by judicial decision will be accepted as authoritative in cases similar to those from which such principles were derived] has special force on questions of statutory interpretation, and Congress had expressed no dissatisfaction with either the *Runyon* or *Griggs* decisions. Thus, it is difficult to characterize these decisions as a product of anything other than a retrenching of the civil rights agenda. In the past 35 years, we truly have come full circle.

Where do we go from here?

We must do more than dwell on past battles, however. The important question now is where the civil rights struggle should go from here.

One answer, I suppose, is nowhere at all—to stay put. With the school desegregation and voting rights cases and the passage of Federal anti-discrimination statutes, the argument goes, the principal civil rights battles already have been won, the structural protections necessary to assure racial equality over the long run are in place, and we can trust the Supreme Court to ensure that they remain so.

This argument is unpersuasive for several reasons. Affirmative action, no less than the active effort to alleviate concrete economic hardship, hastens relief efforts while the victims are still around to be helped. To those who claim that present statutes already afford enough relief to victims of ongoing discrimination, I say, look to the case of Brenda Patterson. She alleged that she had been victimized by a pattern of systematic racial harassment at work, but was told by the Supreme Court that, even accepting her allegations as true, Federal statutory relief was unavailable.

We must avoid complacency for another reason. The Court's decisions during the 1988-89 term put at risk not only the civil rights of minorities, but of all citizens. History teaches that, when the Supreme Court has been willing to shortchange the equality rights of minority groups, other basic personal civil liberties like the rights to free speech and personal security against unreasonable searches and seizures also are threatened.

We forget at our peril that, less than a generation after the Supreme Court held separate to be equal in *Plessy v. Ferguson*, it held in the *Schenck* and *Debs* decisions that the First Amendment allowed the U.S. to convict under the Espionage Act persons who distributed anti-war pamphlets and delivered anti-war speeches. It was less than a decade after the Supreme Court upheld the internment of Japanese citizens that, in *Dennis v. United States*, it affirmed the conviction of Communist Party agitators under the Smith Act. On the other side of the ledger, it is no coincidence that, during the three decades beginning with *Brown v. Board of Education*, the Court was taking its most expansive view not only of the equal protection clause, but also of the liberties safeguarded by the Bill of Rights.

That the fates of equal rights and liberty rights are intertwined inexorably was never more apparent than in the opinions handed down during the 1988-89 term. The right to be free from searches which are not justified by probable cause was dealt yet another heavy blow in two drug testing cases, *National Treasury Employees Union v. Von Raab* and *Skinner v. Railway Labor Executives' Association*. The scope of the right to reproductive liberty was called into considerable question by the *Webster* decision. Although the right to free expression was preserved in several celebrated cases, it lost ground, too, most particularly in *Ward v. Rock Against Racism*, which greatly broadened the government's power to impose "time, place and manner" restrictions on speech.

Looming on the horizon are attacks on the right to be free from the state establishment of religion. In a separate opinion in the creche-and-menorah case, *Allegheny Co. v. American Civil Liberties Union*, four members of the Court served notice that they are ready to replace today's establishment clause inquiry with a test that those who seek to break down the wall between church and state will find far easier to satisfy. We dare not forget that these, too, are civil rights, and that they apparently are in grave danger.

The response to the Court's decisions is not inaction. The Supreme Court remains the institution charged with protecting constitutionally guaranteed rights and liberties. Those seeking to vindicate civil or equality rights must continue to press the Court for the enforcement of constitutional and statutory mandates. Moreover, recent decisions suggest alternate methods to further the goals of equality in contexts other than judicial forums.

For example, state legislatures can act to strengthen the hands of those seeking judicial redress. A lesson of the *Richmond* case is that detailed legislative fact-finding is critical. Civil rights lawyers will stand a far better chance in Federal constitutional litigation over affirmative action if they are armed with a state legislature's documented findings of past discrimination in a particular area. Thus, persons interested in the cause of racial equality can ensure that legislators have access to empirical studies and historical facts that will form the bedrock of acceptable factual findings.

Most importantly, there is Congress. With the mere passage of corrective legislation, Congress can regain in an instant the ground which was lost in the realm of statutory civil rights. By prevailing upon Congress to do so, we can send a message to the Court—that the hypertechnical language games played by the Court in its interpretations of civil rights enactments are simply not accurate ways to read Congress' broad intent in the civil rights area.

Let me emphasize that, while we need not and should not give up on the Supreme Court and while Federal litigation on civil rights issues still can succeed, in the 1990's, we must broaden our perspective and target other governmental bodies as well as the traditional protector of our liberties. Paraphrasing Pres. Kennedy, those who wish to assure the continued protection of important civil rights should "ask not what the Supreme Court alone can do for civil rights; ask what you can do to help the cause of civil rights." Today, the answer to that question lies in bringing pressure to bear on all branches of Federal and state governmental units, including the Court, and urging them to undertake the battles for civil liberties that remain to be won. With that goal as our guide, we can go forward together to advance civil rights and liberty rights with the fervor we have shown in the past.

II. AFFIRMATIVE ACTION PROSPECTS IN THE NEW MILLENNIUM

EDITOR'S INTRODUCTION

It has been projected that by the year 2000, women, minorities and immigrants together will comprise a majority of the American workforce. What awaits them are dramatic changes in American business brought on by the need to maintain industrial preeminence amid mounting worldwide competition. More will be demanded of workers than ever before: they will have to be better educated and more skilled than their predecessors. These requirements of the workplace will take the affirmative action debate to another level. The articles in this section describe the changing demographics of the American workforce, their effects on affirmative action policies, and how corporations and other institutions are attempting to cope with these changes.

One theme that reverberates throughout the articles in this section is that in the future, affirmative action will no longer be merely a function of governmental compulsion, or even a result of moral conviction, but a reaction to economic necessity.

The first selection, "Opportunity 2000," prepared for the United States Department of Labor, surveys the major demographic trends that will effect the American workplace. The second article, written by Sheryl Hilliard Tucker and Kevin D. Thompson for *Black Enterprise* magazine, describes the problems women and minorities face at work and some of the innovative ways corporations are dealing with diversity in the new workforce. Finally, "Is Affirmative Action Still the Answer?" is Robert K. Landers' analysis of the effects of affirmative action on the economic progress of African-Americans. He posits that in the future affirmative action will become less important for blacks than education and job training.

OPPORTUNITY 2000: CREATIVE
AFFIRMATIVE ACTION STRATEGIES
FOR A CHANGING WORKFORCE[1]

The American Labor Market's Emerging Challenge

Challenge is no stranger to American businesses. Our economy has survived depressions, world wars, government manipulation, and natural disasters with amazing resiliency.

But in the midst of mounting worldwide competition that threatens American economic preeminence, our nation's businesses face a unique confluence of important economic forces that could cripple their ability to compete in the years ahead.

These forces and the challenges they present were described in the Hudson Institute's pathbreaking study, *Workforce 2000.* American businesses now and for the remainder of the 20th Century will face a dramatically different labor market than the one to which they have been accustomed for many decades. Traditional sources of labor are rapidly shrinking. And many members of the potential "new workforce"—women, minorities, the economically disadvantaged, disabled—face significant hurdles to their full and effective participation in the workplace. Businesses will be able to satisfy their labor needs only if they successfully confront those barriers and empower individuals presently outside the economic mainstream to take advantage of meaningful employment opportunities.

These changes mean that the ability of companies to effectively compete in the years ahead will be determined in large measure by their success in employing productive workers in a labor market characterized by scarcity, skills deficiencies, and demographic diversity. The most successful companies will be those that meet this challenge creatively and aggressively.

This study reports the findings of a survey of hundreds of companies that was launched to identify the most successful corporate efforts to date in employing the new workforce. These efforts go beyond traditional recruitment efforts—indeed, in

[1]Excerpt of a report prepared for the Employment Standards Administration, U.S. Department of Labor, and submitted by the Hudson Institute, September 1988.

their efforts to attract women, minorities, and others who have been outside the economic mainstream, they surpass even typical notions of "affirmative action." For many of these companies, these efforts mean the difference between a productive and efficient workforce on the one hand and economic disaster on the other.

Most of the efforts cited in this study can be duplicated or adapted by other companies to fit their own particular circumstances. And while many of the businesses profiled are large, their creative efforts to employ the new workforce can usually be replicated in smaller scale or through cooperative efforts with other businesses, trade associations, and community groups.

Before proceeding to these specific corporate efforts, however, it is helpful to review the major trends that will affect the workforce for the duration of this century. Afterward, we will discuss the framework from which firms can most effectively confront these challenges. From this foundation, companies can assess and employ the strategies that can best help them turn challenge into opportunity.

Eight Major Trends That Will Revolutionize Tomorrow's Workforce

In the imagined 21st century workplace of the less sanguine futurologists, machines overtake humans to run every business and institution in the society. Despite advances in technology, that vision is, thankfully, far-fetched. Yet we cannot deny that, in the final years of the 20th century, some profound changes are taking place in the workplace and in the economy.

It is clear that the United States' economy is rapidly entering a new phase, one that has not arrived overnight but is, nevertheless, dramatically different from the post-World War II era in which many workers grew up and began their careers. During that rebuilding period, when hundreds of servicemen and women returned home and optimism was the prevailing sentiment, the United States enjoyed a resurgence of construction, manufacturing, education—and childbearing. By its sheer numbers, the "baby boom" generation that resulted, representing nearly half the increase in the U.S. labor force between 1965 and 1975, came to significantly affect—and continues to affect—the composition of the workplace and nearly every other aspect of American life.

As the baby boom generation now approaches middle age, the fruits of that era—its technological advances, widening opportunities, and changing priorities—have begun to manifest themselves in a number of important changes in the labor force. For example, where once the U. S. workforce was largely dominated by white men, today an increasing number of women and minorities of both sexes have entered the professions and upper management. Where once high school and college students competed for scarce part-time jobs, today there is a surge of "help wanted" signs and appeals to the recently retired. Where once reputable companies could have their pick of a large pool of outstanding potential employees, today, for the first time in more than 20 years, many employers are experiencing a genuine shortage of qualified applicants to match their job openings.

It is clear that between now and the end of this century, American businesses will need to prepare for the inevitable changes in our country's labor supply, as several resourceful and forward-looking companies already have. As they do, here are some of the factors they will have to confront:

Fact 1. The Number of Workers Will Fall

An East Coast drug store chain leaves many of its part-time positions open because of a lack of applicants. "There is definitely an employment problem," says the company's corporate vice president for human resources. "We feel it very acutely in certain areas and for certain jobs. It is difficult to have an adequate applicant stream even to fill a job."

Atlanta fast-food restaurants have been offering new employees nearly double the minimum wage and increasing paychecks early for the best employees to prevent them from leaving.

A survey of Washington, D. C. retailers showed that most area stores were having trouble enlarging their staffs, as usual, for the Christmas rush. "It's been difficult to find employees for the last four or five years," says the manager of one upscale department store, adding that competition among retailers to find employees is fierce.

Scenarios like these will undoubtedly become more common as the United States moves into the 1990s. Businesses that historically have relied on a young workforce—fast-food establishments as well as hotels, amusement parks, and other seasonal enterprises—will need to change the way they recruit and hire. A recent analysis by Morgan Guaranty Trust Company predicts that, in the 1990s, many employers "will find themselves in the unaccustomed position of scrambling for workers."

Why are companies having so much trouble finding the young people to fill the jobs that become available? The problem lies not so much in a new unwillingness by these young workers to accept the pay and opportunities offered to them, but in the shrinking number of young job seekers. As *Workforce 2000* documents, between now and the year 2000, the number of young workers aged 16 to 24 will drop by almost two million, or eight percent. Nor should this development come as such a surprise. As long ago as the late 1970s, schools in a number of metropolitan areas were closing, selling the empty buildings for conversion to office complexes or senior citizen housing, because the number of students had fallen so sharply from earlier years.

Interestingly, it is the baby boom generation that deserves much of the "blame" for the current shortage of young workers. This generation's low fertility rate has, in fact, contributed as much to the upcoming labor shortage as its youthful ranks contributed, not long ago, to a labor surplus. Confounding government planners, who designed programs like Social Security and Medicare, on the expectation that each generation would be larger than its predecessor, the baby boomers decided to have fewer—not more—children than their parents had.

As this generation entered the job market in the 1960s and 1970s, the "boomers" found themselves in keen competition with others of their age. Many ended up with jobs far less stimulating or economically rewarding than they had hoped and expected, given their level of education. At the same time, augmenting the army of workers the population boom brought into the economy during this 20-year period, major social changes opened the door to wider workforce participation by minorities and by women, many of whom were entering the job market for the first time. The economy continued to grow as well, but often not as fast as the ranks of new job applicants. As a result, many baby boomers found the kind of upward mobility their parents had experienced to be an elusive goal. The assurance of steady pay increases also was eroded both by slower wage growth overall and by rising taxes and inflation. For example, even with more and more two-earner couples, the real after-tax income for families headed by a person aged 25 to 34 declined by 2.3 percent between 1961 and 1982. The level of perceived economic security in many families thus fell far below expectations and, as a result, these families

consciously chose to bring fewer children into the world—or to
have no children at all.

Moreover, more women of the baby boom generation finished
college and moved into careers, delaying marriage and children.
Naturally, fewer marriages and a high divorce rate took its toll on
the growth of new families as well. As author Phillip Longman
points out in a recent *Wall Street Journal* article entitled, "The
Downwardly Mobile Baby Boomers," this combination of social
changes and thwarted financial expectations turned the "baby
boom" into a "baby bust." From a high of 3.77 children per
woman in 1957, U.S. fertility in 1972 had fallen below the "replacement rate" of 2.1. In the years since, the rate has averaged
about 1.8.

In sum, based on current trends, the United States' overall
population is expected to reach 275 million by the year 2000, a 15
percent increase over 1985. This rate of increase—approximately
one percent per year during the 1980s and 0.75 percent a year
during the 1990s—indicates that, by the 1990s, the U.S. population will be growing more slowly than at any time in the nation's
history, with the exception of the decade of the Great Depression,
when the rate was also about 0.75 percent per year.

Mirroring the nation's slowly growing population, the labor
force is also expected to increase more slowly than at any time
since the 1930s. Between 1980 and 2000, for example, U.S. government statistics predict that the labor force will grow by about
32 percent: from 107 million to 141 million. By contrast, the labor
force increased by 53 percent between 1960 and 1980.

Of course, the next decade's population growth trends will
affect the number of new entrants into the labor force after the
21st century's opening, but two-thirds of the people who will be at
work by the year 2000 already are employed today, and *all* of
those destined to join the workforce between now and 2000 already have been born. A portion of these new workers will be
young workers; some will be mothers returning to the workplace;
others will be newly trained disadvantaged or disabled job
seekers. And many will be new immigrants.

FACT 2. THE AVERAGE AGE OF WORKERS WILL RISE

Young workers, as companies are already seeing, will become
a less plentiful commodity as the 21st century approaches. Yet the
baby boomers will remain on the job in full force. Between now

and the year 2000; therefore, the number of workers between the ages of 35 and 54 will increase by more than 25 million, and the median age for employed Americans will rise to 39 years, up from 36 in 1987.

An older workforce will affect the economy in both positive and negative ways. On the positive side, a more experienced, stable, reliable, and generally healthy workforce should increase stability and improve productivity in business and industry. The investment employers made ten to fifteen years ago in training these workers should provide dividends for many years to come. Moreover, with a large proportion of the population in its prime earning years, the strain on government support programs should ease and both employees and policymakers should have a better opportunity to plan ahead for the coming deluge of baby boomer retirements.

Mature workers also are more likely to save or invest money than their younger counterparts. A huge increase in the number of workers over age 40 could spur the national savings rate, leading to lower real interest rates and more new investment—another boon to the economy.

On the negative side, an older workforce may be less willing to adapt to changes or take the kinds of risks necessary for rapid financial growth. For example, for an older manager—much more so than for a younger person—physical relocation can mean the disruption of long-established community ties, particularly where family members are involved. A middle-aged person who has invested a number of years in a particular occupation also is more likely than a young worker to have difficulty switching careers.

Another potential problem: many baby boom-aged workers will find themselves "stuck" at the middle-manager level, competing with other members of their generation for scarce promotions. As technology reduces the need for mid-level employees, this group is bound to feel an even greater squeeze.

In addition, more older Americans probably will delay retirement by the year 2000, or even return to the labor force after their retirement. Medical advances and a more health-conscious society are making ages 65, 70, and beyond considerably younger in practical terms than they once were. Examples of older workers staying on the job abound. For instance, in 1986, at the age of 80, acclaimed architect Philip Johnson was still designing multi-million dollar office buildings in Houston, Los Angeles, Washington, D.C., and London. Frank H. Wheaton, Sr., of Wheaton Glass Company, served as the Company's Chairman of the Board until his death in 1986 at age 100. His son, Frank Wheaton, Jr., the company's current President and Chairman, is in his 70s.

Retirement-age workers have been increasingly in demand by businesses that once relied on the young. Fast-food restaurants, supermarkets, and day-care centers are now competing to hire these older adults. In Richmond, Virginia, for example, a major supermarket recruits senior citizens to help bag groceries, load them into cars, and keep shopping carts in order. And a national chain of child-care centers employs close to 2,000 persons aged 55 or older and is starting to recruit through organizations for the elderly. "There is no doubt that this is a labor pool that will be turned to increasingly in the future," says Dr. Marjorie Honig, a professor of economics at Hunter College in New York City.

Aside from the satisfaction older people may derive from remaining in the workforce past age 65, many are also realizing that the decline in younger age groups will make youth-supported programs like Social Security and Medicare much less dependable. Continued employment allows them to take direct responsibility for their financial security.

FACT 3. MORE WOMEN WILL BE ON THE JOB

Any American who owned a television set in the 1950s and 1960s would recognize the "all-American" family portrayed on such programs as "The Adventures of Ozzie and Harriet," "Leave it to Beaver," "Father Knows Best," and "The Donna Reed Show." In these prime-time programs, Father worked in an office while Mother stayed home to take care of the family's suburban home and raise two or three clean-cut youngsters. While this scenario by no means accurately portrayed every American household, it did closely reflect the lives of a majority of women in this country, as fewer than 35 percent of American women worked outside the home in 1950, and, in 1960, fewer than 40 percent of them did.

But the situation has changed markedly over the last 20 years, with the gender balance expected to shift still further before the end of the century. Initially, social change during the late 1960s and early 1970s, coupled with genuine financial necessity, allowed women to gain a foothold in the business world, essentially redefining their role to include paid employment as a norm rather than an exception. Thus, between 1965 and 1975, women increased their representation in the civilian labor force from 39 to 46 percent, a rate that rose to 50 percent by 1985. In 1984, 61 percent of all married women with children were in the labor force—more than twice the 1960 rate of 28 percent—while, in 1985, 54 percent of all mothers of children under age six held jobs outside the home, up from 19 percent in 1960.

These trends will persist for the remainder of the century. Thus, between 1985 and 2000, white males, who only a generation ago made up the dominant segment of the labor market, will comprise only 15 percent of the net additions to the workforce. The majority of new entrants will be women and minorities. By the year 2000, about 47 percent of the workforce will be women, and 61 percent of all American women will be employed.

Despite their growing visibility in the workplace, however, women continue to be concentrated, in nearly the same proportion today as in the 1960s, in "traditionally female" occupations—such as clerical work, elementary school teaching, nursing, and housekeeping—that pay less than men's jobs. As a result, in 1987, the average, full-time working woman still earned only 70 cents to every dollar earned by the average working man.

Such aggregate differences in pay are gradually diminishing, as women increase their numbers in occupations until recently considered "traditionally male." By 1986, for example, 45 percent of full-time accountants and auditors in this country were women, up from 34 percent in 1979. Women also increased their representation in the legal profession from ten to 15 percent; from 28 to 40 percent in computer programming; from 22 to 29 percent in management and administration; and from four to nine percent in electrical and electronic engineering. These proportions should increase even more in the coming years to reflect the growing number of women graduating from professional schools. In 1983, for example, 45 percent of those receiving accounting degrees, 36 percent of new lawyers, 36 percent of computer science majors, and 42 percent of business majors were women.

As women constitute larger and larger percentages of the workforce, predicts Peter Morrison, a demographer at Rand Corporation, "jobs by men and women will be very much alike" with shrinking pay differentials. One Rand study projects that women's wages will equal 74 percent of men's by the year 2000. "The *best* people are going to be very much in demand," Morrison adds, "both men and women."

As a 1986 Equal Employment Opportunity Commission report confirms, women are advancing more rapidly in high-growth, "high-tech" industries than in the older, declining industries. Says Sandra Gunn of Lotus Development Corporation, who has started two new divisions in her first four years with the company: "When you're growing at 500 percent a year, you grab whoever walks in the door who can get the work done."

As we will discuss later, women's large-scale return to the labor force has already caused some companies to rethink their personnel strategies. Wishing to attract and hold valuable female employees, a number of employers are becoming more flexible and innovative in their administration of hours and company benefits, particularly those related to raising a family.

FACT 4. ONE-THIRD OF NEW WORKERS WILL BE MINORITIES

By the year 2000, members of American minority groups—especially blacks and Hispanics—will be less of a "minority" in the workplace than ever before. Over the next several years, almost a third of all new entrants into the labor force will be minorities—twice their current share. Approximately eight million black Americans were in the workforce in 1965; that number increased to 9.3 million in 1975 and 12.4 million in 1985. Although statisticians only recently have begun counting the Hispanic population separately, Hispanics have almost doubled their numbers in the workforce between 1975 and 1985, growing from 4.2 million in 1975 to 6.1 million in 1980, to 7.7 million in 1985.

Minorities will continue to increase their representation in the labor market over the next 20 years for yet another reason: both the black and Hispanic populations in this country have grown more rapidly—both through immigration and high birth rates—than has the white population. Between 1970 and 1984, for example, the black population rose a net average of 15.8 percent a year, compared with 8.3 percent for the white population, and this trend is expected to continue through the end of the century. Another recent Census Bureau report shows the U.S. Hispanic population growing five times faster than the non-Hispanic population.

Black women will comprise the largest share of the increase in the non-white labor force. In fact, by the year 2000, black women will outnumber black men in the workforce, a striking contrast to the pattern among whites, where men outnumber women. Young black women already have surpassed their male counterparts in higher education and occupations requiring advanced degrees. For example, a 1986 Census Bureau report estimated that 770,000 black women in the 25–54 age group were college graduates, while only 633,000 black men of that age group had finished college. National Black MBA Association president Leroy Nunery has estimated that 60 percent of all black MBAs in the U.S. are women, and a College Board study found that, in recent years, gains by black women in such fields as accounting, engineering and law have far exceeded those by black men.

Despite these impressive strides by black women, there are still many minority workers—both men and women—who continue to suffer disadvantages in education and training that may prevent them from moving into the new jobs that are becoming available. Moreover, blacks and Hispanics are overrepresented in industries that are losing jobs, and underrepresented in the most rapidly growing occupations.

Further complicating matters, a large number of minority youngsters—tomorrow's workforce—are still born in poverty. For example, according to Harriette McAdoo, a Howard University social work professor, many highly educated, successful black men and women are foregoing marriage and children, such that the largest proportion of black children are born into less-educated, less-affluent families. The Census Bureau reports that even in the mid-1980s, out-of-wedlock births represented the fastest growing segment of the black population.

FACT 5. THERE WILL BE MORE IMMIGRANTS THAN ANY TIME SINCE WWI

As the destination of choice for those seeking economic opportunity or political refuge, the United States has always been a nation of immigrants, and this is as true in the 1980s as it was in the early 20th century, when millions of European refugees crossed the ocean to begin new lives in America. Although often viewed with suspicion or even hostility by native-born citizens, immigrants have contributed immeasurably over the years to the nation's economic development and cultural richness. British and Irish settlers mined our natural resources; German and Russian refugees worked in garment factories; and Irish, Chinese, Italian, and Slavic immigrants built the nation's extensive railroad network.

Recent immigrants, about a third more than entered the country during the 1960s, have come primarily from Latin America and Asia, the majority of them settling in California, Texas, and New York. Despite language and cultural differences equally as— or even more—profound than their European predecessors, these new residents are quickly finding their niche in American society, some as entrepreneurs, some as workers in family businesses, but nearly all those of working age as members of the labor force.

Between 1970 and 1980, the foreign-born population of the United States increased by about 4.5 million, and approximately 450,000 more immigrants are expected to enter the United States yearly through the end of the century. Immigration at this rate would add about 9.5 million people to the U.S. population and four million people to the labor force. If illegal immigration also continues at recent rates—about 750,000 per year—total immigration would add 16.1 million to the population and 6.8 million to the labor force. Of course, changes in immigration laws or an unexpected influx of refugees from war-torn countries could alter this forecast.

Today's immigrants represent a wide range of social and educational backgrounds. Of adults who entered the United States in the 1970s, 25 percent had less than five years of school, compared to three percent of native born Americans. On the other hand, 22 percent of 1970s' immigrants were college graduates, compared with 16 percent of natives. But regardless of background, most immigrants share a strong determination to better themselves, and it is not uncommon to see new immigrants holding down two or three low-paying jobs at once.

Better educated and trained immigrants often find it discouragingly hard to find jobs that use their skills. For example, one college-educated history teacher from Nicaragua cleans houses for $100 a week. "I worked so hard for my education," she says. "Now, here, I have a language barrier." An Ethiopian man with both a bachelor's and master's degree from American universities is still driving a cab, though he has applied for dozens of jobs in business management.

Despite their difficulties, immigrants seem to attract complaints that "the foreigners are taking away the jobs" from native-born Americans. But several recent studies conclude otherwise, suggesting that legal immigration stimulates, rather than hinders, economic growth. For example, in the Los Angeles labor market during the 1970s, where more than a million foreign-born settled during that period, more jobs were created and unemployment was lower than in the nation as a whole. Another study, released in early 1988, concluded that "immigrants have been absorbed into the American labor market with little adverse impact on natives"—not even on young blacks and Hispanic-Americans, who work in many of the same occupations as new immigrants. "Sometimes I see people who resent the foreign-born," says one county job training director. "[But] we'd be in straits without them."

New immigrants tend to accept lower-paying, less prestigious jobs than the native born: cleaning houses, supervising children, busing tables, or sweeping streets. "No matter how hard it is," says a Cambodian refugee who works at two janitorial jobs, "it's not hard for me. I worked in a communist labor camp from morning until it was so dark you couldn't see the ground anymore." The owner of a custodial service in Reston, Virginia, began hiring Central and South American immigrants when she couldn't find teenagers to fill the jobs. "Before, people quit for the same reasons you or I would quit: The work is boring, demeaning, and all those things you don't want in a job. But most of these people are trying to improve themselves. I know many of them are thinking, 'I don't want to be a janitor for the rest of my life. But this is a start.'"

FACT 6. MOST NEW JOBS WILL BE IN SERVICES AND INFORMATION

Since Eli Whitney invented the cotton gin in the 1790s, Americans have been at the forefront of labor-saving technologies. Almost 200 years later, that talent for technological innovation is leading the United States to the next step along the road of economic development: the transformation into a predominantly service-oriented economy. As the 21st century arrives, in fact, U.S. manufacturing will comprise a small share of the economy—less than a fifth of the GNP—and all net *new* jobs will be in the service sector.

We are already witnessing the beginning of this transformation. The early 1980s brought plant layoffs in older American mining and manufacturing industries while "high tech" enterprises on the west coast boomed. High-priced "consultants" selling knowledge and contacts have become almost as familiar in Washington D.C. as company representatives selling tangible products.

Such a transition is to be expected. Over the years, economists have identified three distinct phases that all modern societies appear to go through: an agricultural phase, followed by an industrial phase, followed by a service phase. Prior to the 1890s, for example, the United States was predominantly an agricultural nation, with approximately half its workforce employed in farming, forestry, or fishing. Then the industrial revolution shifted about 20 percent of the population to the cities—and 15 percent of the nation's workers to manufacturing jobs. Many Latin American and African nations still have predominantly agricultural economies; a number of Asian countries have recently moved into the industrial phase.

But there is more behind the increase in services and decline of manufacturing than just economic theory. New technologies, which require less manual labor to produce a product, have made manufacturing much more productive in recent years. The government's efforts to deregulate some markets has helped stimulate competition and innovation in a number of once-lethargic industries.

While more productive workers will increase America's volume of manufactured goods, their value still is increasing more slowly than the Gross National Product. In other words, whereas manufacturing produced some 30 percent of all U.S. goods and services in 1955 and 21 percent in 1985, its share will drop to less than 17 percent by 2000. And as this trend continues, manufacturing will become less and less important to the economy as a mechanism for creating wealth. It seems ironic that productivity gains, not Japanese competition, are responsible for gradually eliminating manufacturing jobs. But while there will be fewer manufacturing jobs in 2000, these losses should be much more than offset by net new jobs in the service sector. Between now and the year 2000, service industries will create all the new jobs, and most of the new wealth.

Service industries, by definition, create economic value without producing a tangible product. And as factories become more mechanized and automated, a greater percentage of each product's value can be attributed to various services occurring both before and after the product is actually manufactured. Product research and design, market research, engineering, tooling, transportation, wholesaling, retailing, and advertising: these functions can employ more people overall—and at higher wages—than the factories that produce the tangible product.

America's business and government leaders can respond to these inevitable economic developments by taking advantage of the many opportunities for continued progress. How they meet this challenge today will strongly influence both America's long-term prosperity and the well-being of America's labor force.

FACT 7. THE NEW JOBS WILL REQUIRE HIGHER SKILLS

What do a nurse in a large Philadelphia hospital, an assembly-line worker in a New Jersey plastics factory, the manager of a supermarket in northern California, a financial analyst in Boston, and a legal secretary in Houston have in common? Within the last five to ten years, they have all learned to use new forms of computerized equipment on the job. Whatever the occupation, technological innovation has already made it necessary for workers to constantly update and adapt their skills.

In a sense, the American workplace is getting simpler, as technological improvements make it more streamlined and more productive. Computerized equipment allows manufacturing firms to produce a greater number of products with fewer employees. The same is true in offices, where managers learn to use computers and word processors, reducing the need for clerical help. Technology then eliminates many lower skilled jobs, and replaces them with jobs requiring more sophisticated skills and education. Companies thus find themselves requiring more highly skilled workers.

Also contributing to this demand for more highly skilled workers is that today's companies are producing much higher quality products and services in order to compete with foreign manufacturers. David A. Garvin, a professor at the Harvard Business School and the author of *Managing Quality*, says there is a "profound change" in the way U.S. companies are thinking about product quality. "Historically, quality was only a production idea, but in the last decade it has become a marketing concept. We've moved from a view that says quality isn't just a problem to be solved to one that says it's a competitive opportunity."

The 21st century labor force will not only need to adapt to new technologies, but to a new distribution of jobs as well. The vast majority of new jobs will be in service occupations, most requiring post-secondary education. For example, in the year 2000, the labor market will demand 71 percent more lawyers than in 1984. Jobs for scientists—whether in natural, computer, or mathematical sciences—will increase by 68 percent. Jobs in health diagnosis and treatment will jump 53 percent; 44 percent more jobs will be available for technicians; and 40 percent more will open for social scientists. Mining, agriculture, forestry and fisheries, and manufacturing occupations all will lose jobs before the end of the century.

It is easy to see why more than half of all new jobs created over the next 20 years will require some education beyond high school, and that almost a third will be filled by college graduates.

While most new jobs—especially those in the fastest growing categories—will demand much higher language, math and reasoning skills than many current jobs, the opposite is true for slower-than-average-growth job categories. This means that the lowest-skilled workers will be eligible for only about four percent of all new jobs, compared with nine percent of all jobs today.

There will still be a number of jobs created in the services field for medium- to low-skilled workers: cooks, nursing aides, waiters, janitors, secretaries, clerks, and cashiers, to name a few. But even lower-skill occupations will require workers who can read and understand written instructions, add and subtract, and express themselves clearly.

For example, assembly line workers in many manufacturing plants are learning statistical process control, a system that is beyond the reach of those without a solid grounding in mathematics. Factory employees "now need to think sequentially on the job," says one manager. "Before the advanced technology, they didn't have to think as much." Unskilled workers will need training to bring them to the minimum level.

FACT 8. THE CHALLENGE FOR BUSINESS WILL BE IMMENSE

Just after the stock market crash of October 1987, a survey by Manpower Inc., a company highly respected for its employment forecasts, noted that 21 percent of American businesses nonetheless were planning to step up hiring. The study concluded that increased productivity and a shortage of young workers was spurring "an increase in the pace of hiring activity."

But, given the developing worker shortage, what must successful companies do to ensure they have the workers they need to produce their products, to provide their services, and generally to conduct business? Managing and maintaining a skilled workforce in the face of the baby bust will require "imaginative" personnel policies, advises Peter Morrison of the Rand Corporation.

In other words, more than ever before, the competitive edge in hiring will depend upon how well companies attract and keep good workers.

Employers must recognize that the labor supply is changing. Organizations from the computer to the trucking industries will be forced to look beyond their traditional sources of personnel— often young, white males—and work to attract minorities and women, and other members of the "new workforce."

For example, women of the baby-boom generation, who are likely to become some of a firm's most experienced, well-trained, and stable employees, are increasingly drawn to companies that accommodate them in their dual role as workers and mothers. Although more than half of all working mothers are employed full time, a recent Gallup poll found that only 13 percent of these women want to work full-time and regular hours. Six of ten working mothers would prefer part-time employment, flexible hours, or stay-at-home jobs, and 16 percent would prefer not to work at all. Employers that understand and act on these needs will have an advantage among potential female employees. Innovations like flexible hours, use of sick leave to care for children, more part-time work, parental leave for both mothers and fathers, and other innovations are not necessarily cheap, but they may be ultimately necessary changes in the structure of work that will accommodate the combination of work and family.

Not only will employers need to find ways to keep well-qualified women on their payroll, they also face the challenge of helping others to become *more* qualified to perform well. With fewer potential workers to choose from, companies will have an expanded, and more expensive, role to play in developing their own workforces. The number of disadvantaged minorities and immigrants who will join the labor force between now and the year 2000 is growing rapidly, and unless educational and cultural gaps can be closed, many of these new workers will be ill-equipped to meet the advancing skill requirements of the new economy. It is in companies' interest to offer training to the disadvantaged, particularly while they are still young, and to later reap the benefits of their investment as these persons' work capacities rise.

A study by Morgan Guaranty sums it up: "Companies that invest heavily in training, which often goes hand-in-hand with emphasis on internal advancement of workers, may well find that the payoff is unusually high. Firms that carefully consider labor supply in making decisions on office and plant locations also stand to profit."

The economic and labor force changes already under way in the United States will require American businesses and industries to revise their thinking in a major way. Companies wishing to hire and retain the most talented workers will need to develop innovative strategies directed toward the "new workforce," who will comprise an increasing share of available labor in the year 2000. As the following chapters will show, many successful U.S. businesses are already moving aggressively in this direction.

How to Survive and Thrive in a Tight Labor Market

The combined impact of labor scarcity and the emergence of the new workforce presents both challenge and opportunity.

America has the chance, for the first time, to make good on its commitment to opportunity. If companies are to meet their labor needs, they will have to broaden the ethnic and gender makeup of their workforces. In other words, "affirmative action" will no longer be primarily a matter of social responsibility or legal compulsion, but of economic necessity.

On the other hand, companies will be faced with the challenge that traditional forms of affirmative action will not be enough. Rather, if our nation's companies are to remain productive and competitive, they must go beyond traditional notions of affirmative action, moving aggressively to remove the practical impediments that prevent people, whatever their color or ethnicity or gender or disability, from taking full advantage of the employment opportunities now available. It means a substantial investment in human capital—the one type of capital that can set us apart from our world competitors.

WILL DIVERSITY=OPPORTUNITY+ ADVANCEMENT FOR BLACKS?[2]

Walter Davis really enjoys running the investment audit department of his company. Even though it was never openly dis-

[2]Reprint of an article by Sheryl Hilliard Tucker and Kevin D. Thompson, staff writers, *Black Enterprise*, 51+, November 1990. Copyright November 1990. The Earl G. Graves Publishing Co., Inc. 130 Fifth Ave., New York, NY 10011. All rights reserved. Reprinted with permission.

cussed, he was sure that people credited his success to affirmative action. However, that never made Davis question his ability to do his job. Then one of his subordinates, an ambitious white female named Delpha, virtually blindsided him in an effort to impress Walter's boss Hank, the director of corporate finance. When he confronted her, Delpha apologized for not keeping him up-to-date on a project that she was working on, but then told Walter that she didn't really think he was interested in that part of the report. She informed him that Hank had asked her directly for the data.

Angered by this blatant disregard for corporate protocol, Walter confronts his boss. Hank agrees that both he and Delpha had gone around Walter and apologized for this mistake. But when Walter indicated that he felt the problem had racial overtones, Hank seemed puzzled. It was then that Walter outlined his suspicions that his bosses didn't really view him as a real contender for promotions or bigger assignments, and that by bypassing his authority, Hank only reinforced this perception.

Fiction or reality? Both. This scenario is part of an eight-part video training program designed to help companies learn how to value and manage the increasingly diverse work force of the 1990s. Based on real-life case studies, the program—titled BRIDGES: Skills for Managing A Diverse Work Force—uses vignettes to foster candid discussions and skills-building training sessions to improve working relationships among minorities, women and white male managers. Unlike many cultural awareness and diversity training films, the BRIDGES program, owned and distributed by BNA Communications in Washington, D.C., does not focus on blatantly stereotypic cultural and gender-oriented traits. Instead, this innovative program explores subtle stereotypes and offers hard-hitting insights on the everyday frustrations of many blacks, women and other minorities who are forced to play out similar racist and sexist scenarios in corporate America everyday.

"The objective of this program," explains Marjorie Leopold, BRIDGES creator and veteran consultant on equal employment opportunity (EEO) issues, "is not only to sensitize companies to the challenges of managing a diverse work force, but to provide managers with concrete skills and resources on how to effectively motivate and develop everyone who works for them, regardless of race, sex or age."

Unfortunately the outcome for the real life "Walter" was not

as promising as depicted in the video. In the module, Walter and
Hank agree to get to know each other better and respect each
other's turf. And, without accusing anyone specifically, Walter
diplomatically discusses his suspicions about his image with his
staff and then lays down the law about how he wants the department to operate. He then reassures his group that as a supportive
manager, he will also help them position themselves for advancement in the company. The real Walter never confronted his boss
or his staff. Soon after this incident he was let go on the basis that
he was perceived as an ineffective manager.

Workforce 2000 Is Today

Managing Diversity. Valuing Differences. Valuing Diversity.
Whatever the name of the initiative may be, corporate America is
slowly waking up to the fact that the changing employee demographics outlined in the landmark Hudson Institute report
"Workforce 2000: Work and Workers For the 21st Century," is
already a reality. The ground-breaking 1987 report forecasted
widespread shortages of skilled labor and pointed out that between 1985 and the year 2000, 85% of the entrants into the work
force will be women, minorities and immigrants. The report also
said that older workers and disabled employees will require more
of their employer's attention.

Despite the fact that this report was issued three years ago, a
recent survey of 645 organizations conducted by the management
consulting firm Towers Perrin and the Hudson Institute, a policy
research firm, revealed that although nearly three out of four
companies noted some level of management concern over the
added complexities of managing a culturally diverse work force,
only 42% have minority recruiting programs in place. Even more
disheartening is the fact that the survey, titled "Workforce 2000
Competing in a Seller's Market: Is Corporate America Prepared?" reports that although 57% of the respondents claim that
diversity issues affect management decisions and corporate strat-
egy, only 29% actually train managers to value diversity.

The report signals that the American business community is
making feeble attempts to synthesize an increasingly diverse work
force. It's obvious that if top management does not firmly believe
that: 1. diversity is a business issue that affects the company's
ability to effectively compete, and 2. comprehensive training programs are necessary to make this happen, then the diversity issue

will disappear like many of the cultural awareness programs of two decades ago.

In the meantime, blacks, women and other minorities are caucusing inside their companies, filing discrimination complaints and offering insight and advice on how to handle this controversial subject. It's not surprising that Honeywell Corp.'s diversity initiative, which included cultural diversity training sessions, was launched in 1987 after an employee survey revealed that minorities and women believed that their advancement in the company was more limited than that of white males. Others, however, are sitting back, waiting to see if the talk of creating a more open corporate culture will eventually die down. Yet both groups know that a big part of their individual futures rest on—to put it quite bluntly—just how ready the American business community is to give a greater piece of the action to managers who aren't white and who aren't male?

Affirming Diversity

It's no longer good enough, say leading authorities on diversity such as R. Roosevelt Thomas, director of the Atlanta-based American Institute For Managing Diversity Inc. at Morehouse College, for companies to wear their affirmative action and equal employment opportunity statistics as badges of commitment to minorities and women. For the past 30 years, companies have tried to enforce affirmative action and EEO policies designed to institutionalize the recruitment, retention and promotion of minorities and women. For some, affirmative action initiatives were developed as a matter of common decency; others proclaimed that EEO made good business sense; but for many, compliance requirements for lucrative government contracts was the overriding impetus.

Regardless of what initiated a company's EEO efforts, even affirmative action's staunchest critics can't deny its success in bringing substantial numbers of black professionals into corporate America since 1970. However, statistics aren't so encouraging when looking at the movement of blacks up the corporate ladder. African-Americans comprise 10.1% of the nation's 112.4-million employed civilians; 6.2% of its nearly 28 million managers and professionals and 8.5% of its 3.3 million technical and related support staff.

In his breakthrough article "From Affirmative Action to Affirming Diversity," which appeared in the March-April 1990 issue of the *Harvard Business Review,* Roosevelt Thomas took a less confrontational approach: "Affirmative action gets the new fuel into the tank, the new people through the front door. Something else will have to get them into the driver's seat. That something else consists of enabling people, in this case minorities and women, to perform to their potential. This is what we now call diversity. Not appreciating or leveraging diversity, not even necessarily understanding it. Just managing diversity in such a way as to get from a heterogeneous work force, the same productivity, commitment, quality, and profit that we got from the old homogeneous work force." The new litmus test of the progressive organizations of the '90s is reflected by not only how well companies recruit and attract minorities and women, but whether or not the company's corporate culture truly respects and promotes people who differ from the majority of managers and executives throughout corporate America.

Even so, says Thomas, whose diversity training seminars are ranked among the top in the country, "You can't manage diversity without a diverse work force and you're going to need affirmative action to get from here to there."

According to Ted Payne, director of Xerox Corp.'s Office of Affirmative Action and Equal Opportunity in Stamford, Conn., companies are still struggling to find ways to enforce their affirmative-action policies—especially in the aftermath of major downsizing. "At Xerox, we have discontinued our practice of tying affirmative action goals with managers' compensation packages because some of the recruitment and retention problems that individual managers experienced had very little to do with their actions, but were inherent within the culture of the organization itself," explains Payne. (David Kearns, Xerox's chairman and former CEO has molded the copier giant into the undisputed leader in the areas of EEO.) Adds Payne, "If the corporate culture isn't ready to embrace the entire diversity concept, then how can you hold an individual accountable to the numerical dictates of affirmative action?"

Surprisingly, some companies are finding less resistance to implementing diversity training from managers than enforcing EEO policies. That's because many white managers never got beyond regarding affirmative action as "preferential treatment" for blacks and women.

Although many companies still seem confused about the real

difference between affirmative action and diversity initiatives, at Honeywell, the lines are clearly drawn in favor of the latter. In an April 1990 edition of the company's employee magazine, Barbara Jerich, director of work force diversity, describes affirmative action as a social justice effort driven by the U.S. government. It generally focuses on target minority groups and is geared toward compliance. In contrast, diverse work force is an inclusive, development-oriented Honeywell concept that aims at the empowerment of all employees.

"Managing diversity well means addressing, simultaneously, the needs of every segment of the employee population, including white males," Jerich is quoted as saying "When we're doing it right, no individual will be advantaged or disadvantaged because of race, sex, creed, geographical origin or any other form of classification."

According to Alan Zimmerle, corporate manager of equal opportunity, valuing differences and affirmative action, at Digital Equipment Corp. in Maynard, Mass., "The concept of 'differences' is broadly defined at Digital, extending beyond race, age, gender, national origin, and language to include the more subtle characteristics of personality, work ethics, lifestyle and educational background. "The purpose of this work," explains Zimmerle, "is to help employees to recognize the importance of individual differences through self-development. By learning about others, we learn about ourselves. In the process, individuals become empowered to view differences as assets and to put these assets to work creatively. This translates into productivity, profitability and competitive advantage."

Observes Payne: "Unfortunately I've seen some companies where the lifeblood of their affirmative-action policies were drained when diversity became the major thrust. The truth was that although many of the white male managers of these companies were uncomfortable with the idea of 'valuing' talents of people who were different, they quickly resolved themselves to the fact that this may be easier than putting their feet to the fire in keeping up with strict affirmative action goals and timetables."

The "Good Old Boy" Factor

According to U.S. Department of Labor statistics, white males now comprise only 45% of America's 112.4 million employed civilians. However, it will be this group that will be forced to make severe changes in their attitudes and work habits as demographic changes hit home.

"There's no way around it," explains Dr. Anna Duran, founder and director of Columbia University's Executive Program on Managing Cultural Diversity, "as a result of any diversity efforts, white males will be required to share valuable resources, rewards, incentives and promotions with a wider range of people than ever before. For some, the reaction may be disappointment, for others, feelings of betrayal and even anger will color their opinions about the fact that the old rules are changing."

Alfred T. Jackson, director of Employee Counseling, Development and Affirmative Action at the National Broadcasting Corp. and adviser to the BRIDGES program agrees: "We are asking white men to change their entire value system. More than likely, a good number will be threatened by the fact that being a white man no longer automatically entitles them to any natural advantages. Therefore, human resource professionals must replace this sense of entitlement with the clear understanding that white men, along with women and minorities, will continue to be rewarded and promoted on a basis of merit as well as how they integrate good diversity management skills within their own areas of authority."

These issues, plus what Joseph Gibbons, director of Towers Perrin's Human Resource Management Center describes as "pure inertia," have limited the number of companies exploring how to improve opportunities for advancement among non-white workers. "Many human resource managers just don't have the status or the ability to get top management excited about diversity issues," says Gibbons. "Some companies believe that business as usual is just fine. The skeptics are saying, 'Why bother? Nothing is really going to change.' And most line managers are too concerned with the bottom line."

IS AFFIRMATIVE ACTION STILL THE ANSWER?[3]

The Supreme Court is taking a "giant step backward," Justice Thurgood Marshall bitterly asserted. But his protest last January was to no avail. By a 6–3 vote, the court ruled unconstitutional a

[3]Excerpts of an article by Robert K. Landers, staff writer, *Editorial Research Reports*, 198–211, April 14, 1989. Reprinted with permission.

Richmond, Va., ordinance setting aside 30 percent of the city's public works contracts for minority-owned firms. Only where a state or local government was trying to rectify the effects of "identified discrimination" might "some form of narrowly tailored racial preference" be necessary, Justice Sandra Day O'Connor wrote for the court's majority. Thirty-six states and 190 cities and counties had minority set-aside programs similar to Richmond's, and many of the governments have begun to re-examine them in the light of the court's decision.

Less than a week before its ruling in *City of Richmond v. J. A. Croson Co.,* the Supreme Court heard arguments in *Wards Cove Packing Co. v. Frank Atonio et al.,* an employment discrimination case that could be "very significant," according to William L. Robinson, dean of the District of Columbia School of Law and former director of the Lawyers' Committee for Civil Rights Under Law. A crucial issue that could be resolved by the court's ruling in this case is whether an employer whose practices have had a statistically "disparate impact" on minorities must prove (as he has in the past) the "business necessity" of his practices, or whether he must merely produce some evidence that the practices serve a legitimate business interest. If, as many anticipate, the court lifts the heavier burden of proof from the employer, the result, in Robinson's view, will be "to insulate the informal discriminatory practices which occur so frequently."

Despite the Richmond ruling and the prospect of another major setback in the *Atonio* case, affirmative action in employment is not likely to disappear any time soon from American life. The Supreme Court has clearly upheld affirmative action in principle, even if the court now seems to be moving to limit its use somewhat. Affirmative action survived the vigorous assault on it by the Justice Department during the Reagan administration, and it is an established fact in both government and big business.

Although it was not the main factor in the enormous progress that black Americans have made in the past half-century, affirmative action has had an effect. The principal beneficiaries have been young black college graduates. But the benefit to them may have proved somewhat mixed. Many blacks in business and academia have come to resent being perceived as "affirmative action hires," that is, as somehow unqualified for, or incompetent at, their jobs. Wrong and even racist as that perception often is, some blacks have ruefully come to regard it as a predictable result of affirmative action.

But whatever its disadvantages, some middle-class blacks did at least benefit from affirmative action. To unskilled blacks trapped in the underclass, however, affirmative action has meant virtually nothing. "It seems to me that affirmative action would be all right if it were designed to help the economically disadvantaged," says Shelby Steele, a professor of English at San Jose State University who has written about race for *Harper's* and *Commentary* and is at work on a collection of essays on the subject. "But any time it's based solely on color or ethnicity or gender, I think it's absolutely wrong and it's going to create backlash and . . . other difficulties."

Steele's view is still apparently a minority one among blacks. Nevertheless, it is evident that affirmative action is a much smaller part of "the solution" for black America than was once imagined, and, indeed, it may even have become a part of "the problem"—a distraction from the real difficulties facing unskilled blacks and irrelevant to the troubling question of why more blacks have not taken advantage of the opportunities that opened up for them as a result of the hard-fought struggle for racial justice.

Affirmative action is, of course, a fruit of that struggle, a symbol of blacks' successful assertion of their rightful claim on the American conscience. "[E]ven though [affirmative action] is not what we really need right now," Steele says, "we cling to it as a symbol of our power, and we feel that to lose it would be to indicate that we've lost power in American life." Others believe that affirmative action is more than a symbol and more even than just an established fact, that it remains a vital tool in the quest for a just and ultimately color-blind society. Whatever the truth of the matter, it is clear that the impassioned debate about affirmative action is not quite over.

Federal Rules, Courts Changed the Meaning

The meaning of affirmative action has changed greatly over the years. As originally used by Presidents Kennedy and Johnson, the term meant that federal contractors would act affirmatively to recruit workers, without discrimination. "'Affirmative action' originally meant that one should not only not discriminate, but inform people one did not discriminate; not only treat those who applied for jobs without discrimination, but seek out those who might not apply," notes sociologist Nathan Glazer. In the Civil Rights Act of 1964, the term "affirmative action" was used to refer to the sort of action—such as hiring or reinstatement of employees, with or without back pay—that a court might order an employer found guilty of discrimination to take. But employers otherwise were explicitly *not* to be required "to grant preferential treatment to any individual or group" on the basis of race (or sex) "on account of an imbalance which may exist with respect to the total number or percentage of persons" of any race (or sex) employed.

In subsequent years, however, affirmative action came to mean something quite different. As a result of interpretations made in federal regulations and court rulings, federal contractors and private employers who had *not* been found guilty of discrimination began to be required to take race (and gender) into account in their hiring and promotions. If their work forces were found to be racially imbalanced, the employers had to establish numerical "goals" to correct the imbalance, along with "timetables" for reaching the goals—and then to make "good faith" efforts to do so. Critics said all this amounted to illegal racial quotas, but advocates of affirmative action (in its new meaning) denied this and insisted that, as Justice Harry A. Blackmun once put it, "In order to get beyond racism we must first take account of race."

With the shift in its meaning, affirmative action became controversial. Critics maintained that the way to get beyond racism in employment was to see to it that employers did *not* take race into account. Employment decisions should be based, as much as possible, on the individual applicant's or employee's ability to perform the job. If the result was less than proportional equality for blacks and whites, then so be it. Equality of opportunity for individuals, no matter what their race, was the object to be achieved, after all, not necessarily equality of result. According to this view, black Americans had made substantial progress and would continue to do so, without the aid of preferential treatment or discriminatory quotas.

Proponents of affirmative action (in its new and current meaning) took a different position. The historical fact of racial discrimination, they contended, had consequences that simply could not be ignored. "There was rigid racial segregation and individual definition of opportunity on the basis of race for hundreds of years," Robinson says. "[If] you proclaim no more discrimination and you inculcate in society broadly the feeling that it is wrong to be motivated by the race of the person with whom you are dealing, that just simply doesn't undo racial discrimination. And if that's all you did, then for the foreseeable future you would essentially have changed the legal status but would have left people where they were. And that's just not a proper response to the fact of racial discrimination as it has occurred in our society. That does not create for us the society of genuine equal opportunity, the non-race-based society that I think even the pro- and anti-affirmative action debaters would agree is the ultimate goal."

There may be agreement about the ultimate goal, but there is sharp disagreement about existing social reality, and that disagreement has underlain much of the debate about the use of affirmative action as a "temporary" means to achieve the ultimate goal. Justice Marshall, in his dissent in the Richmond case, complained that the court majority was signaling "that it regards racial discrimination as largely a phenomenon of the past, and that government bodies need no longer preoccupy themselves with rectifying racial injustice. I, however, do not believe this nation is anywhere close to eradicating racial discrimination or its vestiges."

Other proponents of affirmative action do not believe that, either. To Josh Henkin, assistant editor of the liberal Jewish magazine *Tikkun,* for instance, "[T]he American ideal of meritocracy is a sham. . . . [I]t is absurd to argue . . . that people who achieve academic and career success do so by winning the meritocratic race. The starting line is radically different for different people, and these divergent starting lines all too often reflect racial and sexual divisions." Racism, he thinks, "[goes] a long way toward explaining . . . why a black man with more than an elementary-school education earns 30 percent less than a white man with the same education, and why the black poverty rate is nearly three times as high as the overall poverty rate."

Critics of affirmative action, however, believe that racial discrimination is a far less significant force than it used to be. Glazer points out that the "barriers to economic activity and education [which] had been overwhelming for blacks . . . [were] lifted through the success of the civil rights struggle." Although discrimination, to be sure, did not completely cease to exist, the laws against it "were powerful and powerfully enforced. Blacks . . . made great progress in the 1960s without affirmative action." In his 1975 book, *Affirmative Discrimination,* Glazer cited econometric studies that had found, as one of them put it, that "traditional discriminatory differences in the labor market [were] abating rapidly."

But statistical disparities in the racial composition of work forces continued to exist, and from such disparities, apparent discrimination has been inferred. As the Equal Employment Opportunity Commission (EEOC), one of the main government agencies charged with enforcing affirmative action, asserted in one case, in reference to entry-level jobs: "A substantial underrepresentation of women or minorities in certain job categories manifestly cannot be attributed to their lack of skill. Absent discrimination, one would expect a nearly random distribution of women and minorities in all jobs."

Glazer strongly disagrees with that argument: "Absent discrimination, . . . one would expect nothing of the sort. . . . [The] various elements that contribute to the distribution of jobs of minority groups [include]: level of education, quality of education, type of education, location by region, by city, by part of metropolitan area, character of labor market at time of entry into the region or city, and many others. These are factors one can in part quantify. Others—such as taste or, if you will, culture—are much more difficult to quantify. Discrimination is equally difficult to quantify. To reduce all differences in labor force distribution (even for entry-level jobs) to *discrimination* is an incredible simplification."

Still, some of the other factors that affect job distribution undoubtedly reflect, to some extent, *past* discrimination. "Thus," stated a Wharton Center for Applied Research study group on affirmative action, set up at the request of the U.S. House Committee on Education and Labor, "although current acts of discrimination might be widely condemned as incompatible with contemporary American values, and punished because they are unlawful, the mere enforcement of laws against discriminatory behavior will not assure equal opportunity. Something more is required to secure and protect the right of all persons to participate fully in the economy." The study group went on to cite a statement made by President Johnson in a 1965 speech at Howard University: "You do not take a person who, for years, has been hobbled by chains and liberate him, bring him up to the starting line of a race and then say, 'you are free to compete with all the others,' and still justly believe that you have been completely fair."

Yet to critics of affirmative action, complete fairness also would not include "reverse discrimination," which is what they believed affirmative action had been reinterpreted to be. In their view, special efforts at education or encouragement or recruitment—affirmative action's original meaning—were warranted to increase minority representation in the work place—but not numerical goals, quotas or racial preference. "Until Jackie Robinson broke the color bar in organized sport in the United States, the most virulent kinds of prejudice prevailed against members of minorities," philosopher Sidney Hook observed. "Today who would argue that in compensation for the gross injustices of the past the composition of our basketball, football, baseball, and track teams be determined by any kind of ethnic quota system or numerical ratios reflecting either the relative distribution of ethnic groups in the general population or in the pool of those available? It would be absurd to propose any other criterion except color-blind merit in filling the available posts regardless of what the numerical distribution turns out to be."

Black Middle Class is a Real Success Story

The economic progress made by black Americans in the last half-century has been dramatic. The "real story" of the years since 1940, economists James P. Smith and Finis R. Welch have written, has been "the emergence of the black middle class, whose income gains have been real and substantial." In 1940, more than 75 percent of black men were "destitute, with little hope that their lot or even that of their children would soon improve." Only 22 percent of black men were in the middle class. And the black "economic elite resembled an exclusive white club"—only 2 percent of black men belonged. By 1980, all that had changed: By then, 80 percent of black men were *not* destitute. More than two out of three black men were in the middle class, and membership in the economic elite had swelled to 12 percent. "For the first time in American history, a sizable number of black men [were] economically better off than white middle-class America," Smith and Welch pointed out.

Norton contends that this immense progress would have been "absolutely impossible without affirmative action. There were two things that did it: Businesses [began] to employ people they had routinely turned away before, and schools—some of the best schools and schools of all kinds—opened up to minorities. . . . Blacks did not prepare themselves in the same fields before affirmative action as they do today. . . . [The] most popular college major for blacks [today is] business, because affirmative action has had the effect of opening jobs, [and] young black people think it matters that you get a job if you major in business. The proverbial story all my life was that black men who had college degrees worked in the post office, where white men who had eighth-grade educations worked, because they couldn't get hired [in business or professional jobs] downtown. . . . [Now,] affirmative action [has] had such a high profile that young black people [have] understood that you should go to law school, you can now be hired by a firm; you can go to business school and you [can] get a job in the corporation, [even though] your father could not."

There is no doubt that affirmative action has been effective, Welch says. Skilled and qualified blacks "[have] gotten into larger firms [and] they're being taken much more seriously." He and Smith found that affirmative action "significantly shifted black male employment toward EEOC-covered firms and industries, and particularly into firms with federal contracts. Affirmative action also increased the representation of black male workers in managerial and professional jobs in covered firms." The big shift took place mainly in the late 1960s and was largely over by 1974. During those years, "there was a remarkable surge in incomes of young black males," as firms covered by the EEOC "rapidly increased their demand for black workers, bidding up their wages. However, once the stock of black workers had reached its new equilibrium, this short-run demand increase was completed and wages returned to their long-run levels."

For black men as a whole, affirmative action had no significant long-term impact on their narrowing wage gap with white men, according to Smith and Welch's analysis. The relative improvement after affirmative action was instituted took place (until about 1980) at about the same rate as it had before. The massive migration of Southern blacks to the cities of the North in the decades from 1940 to 1970 was one reason for blacks' economic progress. Education was another. Blacks were not only becoming better educated, but their education was counting for more economically. However, Smith and Welch noted, "the increase in the economic benefits of the black schooling began long before the affirmative-action pressures of [the 1960s and '70s]." Thus, the economists argue, it was "the slowly evolving historical forces" of education and migration that "were the primary determinants of the long-term black economic improvement. At best affirmative action has marginally altered black wage gains about this long-term trend."

Some black Americans did achieve significant economic benefits from affirmative action, however. As might perhaps have been expected, they were mainly young college graduates. In 1967-68, the wages of young black male college graduates had been only about 75 percent of their white peers' wages; four years later, the blacks' wages reached and slightly exceeded the whites'. Once the EEOC-covered firms obtained their targeted numbers of blacks, however, the wage gap began to widen again, so that in 1979, young, black college graduates' wages were 91 percent of the whites' wages. Even so, the wage gap was substantially smaller than it had been just a decade or so earlier—and affirmative action had helped to reduce it.

But affirmative action's beneficiaries have found that its benefits are not inexhaustible. It enabled many blacks and women "to enter occupations and industries from which they had long been excluded," the Wharton study group said. "But . . . [m]any minority and female employees are now in middle-level positions [in private firms] where they feel frustrated about their prospects for promotion. Breaking . . . into higher management and executive positions is especially difficult because of the greater importance of subjective performance measures at that level. . . . Under such circumstances, the failure of minority and women workers to advance in numbers commensurate with their overall participation in the work force sparks cries of discrimination, even when other legitimate factors are involved."

"Most black managers are convinced that their best is never seen as good enough, even when their best is better than the best of white colleagues," notes Edward W. Jones Jr., who is president of his own consulting firm in South Orange, N.J., and a former manager at New York Telephone Co. and at AT&T. "The barrier facing black managers is no less real than a closed door. But in the minds of many of their superiors, if people can't make it on their own, it must be their own fault." Because of people's tendency "to act favorably toward those with skin color like theirs and unfavorably toward those with different skin color," Jones maintains, "many of [the] best qualified managers are seen as unqualified 'affirmative action hires.'" In his view, this is hardly the fault of affirmative action, whose objective is simply "to ensure that all qualified persons compete on a level playing field."

"We ought to get rid of people's attitudes," Norton says, not get rid of affirmative action. Not only does "affirmative action in fact . . . not mean hiring less-qualified people, [but] if you hire less-qualified people, there's a [legal] cause of action. And there are reverse-discrimination suits brought every day that are won. They are very small in number compared to discrimination suits, however."

The perception that a particular black person in business or the professions is an unqualified "affirmative-action hire," may well be inaccurate, unfair and even, in some instances, racist. "But, in any case, certainly that perception does exist and does affect those blacks who, whether through affirmative action or otherwise, have moved ahead," Steele, the San Jose State English professor, says. However, in his view, the perception is a predictable consequence of affirmative action. "[A]ny time you grant affirmative action to people on the basis of color alone, then I think inevitably you're going to diminish the importance of those people who have been let in. I don't think there's any easy way around that. People are going to say, logic following logic, that 'You're here because you're black.' . . . And this is going to be difficult for you, in whatever professional setting it may be."

Steele used to believe affirmative action was fine, but over the years he has gradually changed his mind. "Certainly, as a college professor, it irks me deeply when people perceive or feel that I'm here because of affirmative action. I find that a very demeaning sort of view and resent it deeply. And I think certainly most other blacks also resent it, because the suggestion is, well, you wouldn't be here otherwise or you're incompetent in some way. There's a lot of racial stereotyping that blacks have always endured, [and it] now can pass under this 'affirmative action' label."

Racial discrimination is the real issue, Steel contends. "The goal, obviously, is to get race out of the picture as much as possible, if not to end discrimination. And I think affirmative action, as it's now practiced, probably contributes more to racism than it eradicates it."

Some Blacks Still are Losing Ground

Despite all the progress black Americans have made, too many still remain mired in poverty. The growth of the black middle class is only part of the story. The other part is the emergence of the underclass, which, in political scientist Lawrence M. Mead's description, "comprises those Americans who *combine* relatively low income with functioning problems such as difficulties in getting through school, obeying the law, working, and keeping their families together." The underclass is about 70 percent non-white.

The two trends appear to contradict one another. "Among those [men] who work, there is clear evidence that earnings of blacks are rising relative to whites, but increasing fractions of black men do not work," Welch observes. In 1960, nearly 78 percent of black men in their early 20s were employed or in school. Two decades later, after the great advances in civil rights and the enforcement of affirmative action, only 70 percent were employed or in school. Not only were 12 percent unemployed (about 3 points higher than in 1960), but nearly 13 percent of black men in their early 20s—more than 4 percentage points higher than in 1960—were not in the labor force (that is, not even actively looking for employment). Nearly 5 percent of black men in their early 20s were in jail. As author Charles Murray famously put it, young black males, when compared with young white males, "lost ground."

Ground was lost not only in employment but in education. A report last year by the Commission on Minority Participation in Education and American Life, sponsored by the American Council on Education, said that in higher education "the picture of stalled progress is dramatically clear. During the same period when the pool of minority high-school graduates was becoming bigger and better than ever, minority college attendance rates initially fell, and have remained disproportionately low." The percentage of black high-school graduates in their early 20s who had completed one or more years of college had jumped from 39 percent in 1970 to 48 percent five years later, while the corresponding rate for whites remained steady at 53 percent. But between 1975 and 1985, while the college participation rate for white youths increased to 55 percent, the rate for blacks dropped to 44 percent (before going back up to 47 percent in 1986, which was still less than in 1975). The college participation rate for black males fell even more precipitously.

Not only were not enough blacks going to college, but too many who did were dropping out before graduation. In 1984-85, although blacks made up 9 percent of all undergraduates, they received only 8 percent of the associates' degrees and only 6 percent of the bachelor's degrees conferred that year. At the graduate level, the commission noted, the falloff was dramatic. Between 1976 and 1985, the number of blacks earning master's degrees declined by 32 percent, and the number earning doctorates dropped by 5 percent. "In certain critical fields of study, the minority presence is nearly non-existent," the commission said. In computer science, for instance, only one black received a doctorate out of 355 awarded in 1986. In mathematics that year, blacks received only six of the 730 doctorates awarded.

Opportunity increasingly beckoned, but not as many black Americans seized it as should have. "By most [socioeconomic] measures—infant-mortality rate, teen pregnancy, and so forth—the gap [between blacks and whites] is wider today than it was in the '50s," Steele says. "The startling thing . . . is that just as we have declined, our opportunities have increased. We have certainly a great deal more opportunity today than we did in the 1950s. And yet at the same time, we've had this decline. Well, obviously that points the finger back at us. What kinds of things are going on in black life that account for that kind of decline? We should have at least held even, if not progressed a great deal."

Many factors, including the deterioration of the traditional black family structure, clearly are involved. But Steele says that "in a general sort of way, I think that . . . we have not really looked at our own anxieties about inferiority, our own fear of moving into the mainstream, of taking opportunities, of making efforts to get ahead, and so we've held back and hesitated, and certainly in a competitive society like America, you can't hesitate and hold your ground, you're going to decline, and we have declined."

Steele contends that the "victim-focused black identity" is holding blacks back. "We think of ourselves too much as victims. It makes you more passive, it makes you more demoralized, it robs you of individual initiative. . . . We're so busy seeing ourselves as victims, seeing racists everywhere, that we're unable to see opportunity and simply unable to take advantage of it in the way that we should be taking advantage of it. Because we have an enormous amount of opportunity. Anybody can go to college. Or if [the opportunity is denied], there's an entire body of laws there that you can rely on to seek redress. And we're not doing it, we're not taking advantage."

The employment opportunities for blacks and other minorities are expected to increase in the coming years, thanks to demographic change. "With fewer new young workers entering the work force, employers will be hungry for qualified people and more willing to offer jobs and training to those they have traditionally ignored," the Hudson Institute pointed out in a 1987 study done for the U.S. Labor Department. "At the same time, however, the types of jobs being created by the economy will demand much higher levels of skill than the jobs that exist today." To take advantage of the increased opportunities, then, blacks and other minorities will have to acquire the higher levels of skill. If they don't, affirmative action will be of little help.

"If the policies and employment patterns of the present continue," the institute warned, "it is likely that the demographic opportunity of the 1990s will be missed and that, by the year 2000, the problems of minority unemployment, crime, and dependency will be worse than they are today. . . . Now is the time to renew the emphasis on education, training, and employment assistance for minorities that has been pursued with limited success over the past several decades. These investments will be needed, not only to insure that employers have a qualified work force in the years after 2000, but finally to guarantee the equality of opportunity that has been America's great unfulfilled promise."

For the next 20 years, Robinson says, "the spotlight that emphasizes education, job training, must burn more brightly than it has before, it must burn more brightly than the spotlight of affirmative action. But that is not to say that the spotlight of affirmative action can be immediately turned off. Instead, I think that as it expires, it will do so gradually. It will dim, dim, dim, dim and fade out of the picture, at some point in the future. I don't know exactly when."

For the foreseeable future, affirmative action is here to stay. But it no longer seems to have as much practical significance for black Americans as it once appeared to have. Education and job training clearly are the greater need now. And they, as it happens, were part of what affirmative action originally was all about.

III. HIGHER EDUCATION

EDITOR'S INTRODUCTION

In 1977 Allan Bakke's application for admission to the University of California School of Medicine at Davis was rejected. Rejection letters are common, but Bakke's reaction was not. In a law suit he charged that the University's decision to reject him was in order to fill a minority quota and that had he not been white, he would have been accepted. What resulted from a young man's desire to become a doctor was the landmark Supreme Court case of 1978, *The Regents of the University of California v. Bakke. Bakke* was the first case to challenge the constitutionality of an affirmative action program. However, the Court's decision seemed to deliver a contradictory message: while ruling that Title VI of the 1964 Civil Rights Act prohibited the University from establishing fixed quotas for minorities, the justices went on to say that the Constitution did not bar college admissions offices from introducing race as a factor in its selection process. Thus, Bakke was allowed to enter medical school at UC Davis, and universities and colleges could continue to consider race in college admissions. *Bakke* was only the beginning.

Nowhere are affirmative action policies so controversial as in the world of academia. Competition among applicants, especially for elite colleges and universities, can be keen. Some observers argue that students should be admitted solely on academic merit, while others contend that the need for diversity dictates that other factors be used in the selection process. They point out that many women and white students from economically disadvantaged homes who would not normally attend college have benefitted from affirmative action programs.

This section contains articles that deal with affirmative action on the university level. The first two articles, written by Jayjia Hsia for *Educational Policy,* and James Gibney for *The New Republic,* discuss the special dilemma facing many schools with respect to Asian-American enrollment. The authors explore what can happen when affirmative action goals clash with proportionality. They analyze the reasons behind the trend of restricting Asian-American students access to some of the country's most prestigious universities.

In "Latino Faculty at the Border," Michael A. Olivas, writing for *Change* magazine, gives his views on the inadequate recruitment and retention of the very few Latino law professors. Next, an article in *Time* relates how one frustrated African-American law professor expressed his displeasure with the lack of minority women faculty at Harvard Law School. In the final article, entitled "Exclusive Opportunities," John Bunzel criticizes what he perceives to be discriminatory faculty hiring practices at many of the nation's universities. He warns that racial quotas are increasingly being applied to faculty appointments.

LIMITS OF AFFIRMATIVE ACTION: ASIAN-AMERICAN ACCESS TO HIGHER EDUCATION[1]

The fastest growing minorities on campuses are Asian Americans. Although they are identified demographically as a group, Asian American students are a diverse lot. They represent more than 20 nations and over 60 ethnic groups. Some are fifth-generation Americans; others landed no more than a year or two ago. What is the cumulative impact of two decades of affirmative action in higher education for Asian Americans? Were Asian American students fortunate and timely beneficiaries?

This paper argues that during its first decade, affirmative action probably served as a catalyst for improving access. Widespread commitment to civil rights eased entry to selective institutions and exclusive professions that had been beyond the reach of Asian Americans. However, some Asian subgroups had in fact exceeded their national representative proportions (less than a fraction of 1 percent of the total U.S. population when affirmative action began) in colleges and universities long before affirmative action. They invested in higher education even when there were no jobs open to them as college graduates. By the 1970s, the handful of institutions that included Asian and Pacific Islander Americans in affirmative action programs limited eligibility to students from socioeconomically disadvantaged backgrounds, or

[1]Reprint of an article by Jayjia Hsia, senior research scientist, Educational Testing Service. *Educational Policy* 2:117–36, 1988. Reprinted with permission.

to narrow target groups such as Filipino-Californians or Samoans and Guamanians. Today, virtually no Asian Americans are regarded as viable candidates for student affirmative action programs.

Other forces, concurrent with affirmative action, were responsible for the Asian population explosion on campuses in the United States. These included liberalized federal laws governing immigration and refugees, selective migration, the propensity of Asians to concentrate in metropolitan areas on both coasts, and their deep desire for higher education. Newcomers, even more than acculturated third- and fourth-generation Asian Americans, assiduously honed their academic abilities, maintained consistent records of academic achievement, and persisted in high school through graduation. Moreover, their families willingly sacrificed immediate comforts to invest in quality education for the next generation.

Minorities, including Asian Americans, and women were designated protected groups under affirmative action. But by the late 1970s, the doubling, tripling, even quadrupling of competitive Asian American applicants had strained the willingness of some of the most selective institutions to accommodate more of them. Qualified Asian Americans are now less likely than any other applicants, including Whites, to be admitted by the colleges of their choice, whether that choice is a prestigious Ivy League member or a top West Coast public university.

Consciously or subconsciously, affirmative action goals have been transformed into provisional caps or ceilings. The standard goal, proportional representation based on national population counts, is now used to explain limits on Asian American enrollments. Originally intended to improve access, affirmative action has become a deterrent to equal opportunity. This special issue provides a forum to examine the contradiction between two "goods," proportional representation and equal educational opportunity. For Asian Americans, the notion of proportional representation has not only failed to eliminate bias, but has emerged as a reason for renewed discriminatory treatment based on race. This paper describes how these changes came about and considers their implications.

Changes in the Structure of the Asian American Population

Asians did not emigrate in the nineteenth and early twentieth centuries to seek an education. Most left their homelands to escape war, poverty, famine, and other natural and man-made disasters. Chinese workers first arrived in 1849 and continued until the flow was cut off by the Chinese Exclusion Act of 1882. Japanese, Filipino, and other Asian laborers followed in successive waves as replacements. Each new group of Asians soon became unwelcome competitors in the labor market. The 1924 National Origins Act barred immigrants from Asia altogether, with the exception of Filipinos. Until the Philippine Independence Act of 1934, Filipinos could enter the country freely as United States nationals. Thereafter, Filipino immigration was limited to 50 entrants a year.

Chinese, Japanese, and other Asians were ineligible for citizenship through naturalization. Native-born Asian American children whose parents paid more than their share of taxes were relegated to segregated, inferior schools or denied public education altogether. In some states such discriminatory laws remained on the books until the 1950s. The McCarran-Walter Immigration and Nationality Act of 1952 ended all racial bars to naturalization and gave token quotas of about a hundred immigrants each year to most Asian nations. Preference was given to individuals with training and skills needed by the United States. The Immigration Act of 1965 ended all racial and ethnic quotas. While professionals, scientists, and outstanding artists were still given preference, priority was for family reunification. Asians again began to emigrate in numbers from 1968 onwards, when liberalized Eastern Hemisphere quotas took effect.

New Asian immigrants were very different from the contract laborers of the nineteenth and early twentieth centuries. Sixty-four percent of the new immigrants came from Asia with some college education. They left their homelands for a higher standard of living, to pursue advanced degrees, to seek better jobs; but above all they emigrated to give their children a better chance in life through quality higher education.

Since 1975, successive waves of Southeast Asian refugees have landed through a series of parole authorizations granted by the Attorney General under the Immigration and Nationality Act of 1952 and the Refugee Act of 1980. First-wave Vietnamese refugees were socioeconomically and educationally advantaged. The more recent "boat people" have come from much less privileged circumstances. But with few exceptions these refugees, too, expect their children to go to college.

New immigration and refugee policies, and selective migration have accordingly changed the structure of the Asian American population. Newcomers are now the majority. By 1985, there were more than five million Asian Americans, 2.1 percent of the population. By the turn of the century, the Asian American population is projected to become ten million, or 4 percent of the total population. The effects of these new laws and policies have been far greater than affirmative action programs on Asian American college enrollments.

Even though they are less likely than other applicants to be accepted by their top choice colleges or universities, almost nine out of ten Asian American high school graduates go right on to postsecondary education. Hopes may be dashed, but few give up their aspirations. They enroll in their second or third choice back-up schools, or begin at community colleges with plans to transfer to four-year institutions. Why do newcomers as well as third- and fourth-generation Asian Americans possess such single-minded devotion to higher education? Cultural values certainly play a role. But economic survival remains the driving force. For a century, Asian Americans were excluded from the primary labor market. They were not allowed to ply skills and trades brought from the old country, were denied union membership, and were barred from professions by barriers of language, work permits, licenses, and certification. Investment in higher education was the single way out of the ghetto.

Education is the chief determinant of group differences in earnings. Some Asian Americans are approaching economic parity as a result of overinvestment in education. If typical Asian Indian, Chinese, Filipino, Japanese, or Korean men's educational levels were adjusted downward to match those of the average White male in regional labor pools, Asian American earnings would be several hundred to thousands of dollars lower than White earnings. Better education gains entry to higher status occupations. However, within each occupational category, Asian Americans continue to hold lower-paying jobs. The enduring inequities are subtle in expression, and rest primarily on differential access to institutional settings such as Ivy League colleges, plum public sector jobs, and the fast track at Fortune 500 companies.

The Role of Affirmative Action

Asian Americans were a fraction of 1 percent of the population in the United States as late as 1970. Affirmative action was not needed by most Asian American groups for attaining proportional representation in higher education. The 1950 census recorded that Japanese Californians were the best educated group in the state. By 1960, lingering prejudice and discrimination notwithstanding, median years of schooling of Japanese American males and females, and of Filipino American females, had exceeded the educational levels of White adults of the same sex nationally. That same year, 65 percent of seniors at the University of Hawaii were Japanese Americans. Since they were a smaller fraction of the freshman class three years earlier, their record served as a testimony to Japanese American persistence.

In 1966, when the University of California at Berkeley conducted its first ethnic survey of students in planning affirmative action policies and programs, Asian Americans were already close to 6 percent of the student body. The 1970 census recorded that Asian American groups with above average proportions of adults 25 years and over, and with at least 4 years of college included Koreans, Chinese, Filipinos, and Japanese with 36, 26, 23, and 16 percent, respectively, compared to 12 percent among White adults. By 1980, Asian Americans aged 20 to 24 enrolled in school included Chinese, Japanese, Asian Indian, Vietnamese, Korean, and Filipino Americans with 60, 48, 44, 41, 40, and 27 percent, respectively, compared to White enrollment of 24 percent.

Affirmative action did increase enrollments of qualified Asian Americans to private, highly selective institutions with "academic plus" admissions criteria; facilitated Asian American female access to institutions and fields formerly dominated by White males; and raised the aspirations of peoples accustomed to rejection by mainstream America. During the first decade of affirmative action, institutions were more ready to admit qualified Asian Americans in order to meet overall minority enrollment goals. Affirmative action functioned for Asian Americans as a catalyst to accelerate the pace of change rather than as an opening wedge to postsecondary education.

The Reversal of Affirmative Action

By the mid-1970s, rapid growth of the applicant pool, higher proportions of immigrants and refugees, and competitive qualifications of both newcomers and the native-born threatened prevailing notions of minority performance in relation to standards set by middle-class, college-bound White males. Asian American students were more likely than all other students to graduate from an academic program in high school, attend a four-year college, finish college on schedule, and finance college by their own and family earnings and savings; they were least likely to receive grants or loans. Those who go on to a professional or graduate school were likely to stay the course.

Subtle but rising barriers became apparent toward the late 1970s. The Asian American population continued to change and grow, as did its college applicant pool during a period of declining college-age population nationwide, and stable or falling minority enrollments. However, Asian American admissions did not keep up with demographic trends.

The reversal of affirmative action for Asian Americans can be documented for any institution willing to make public its records on applicants, admitted students, and matriculated students by ethnic groups during the affirmative action years. When Asian Americans were candidates for affirmative action, their admit rates (the ratio of admitted students to applicants) were higher than average. When they were no longer considered for affirmative action, ethnic Asian admit rates became even with overall or White admit rates. When affirmative action goals became provisional lids to contain Asian American enrollment growth, their admit rates fell below White rates. As will be discussed, lower admit rates reflected not only more stringent adherence to existing standards but also the higher qualifications required of admitted Asian Americans.

Overall Asian American admission rates were below average in 1985, according to a national survey of four-year undergraduate institutions. The Asian American admission rate to public institutions was about 92 percent of the total admission rate; to private institutions, 77 percent of the total admission rate. The disparity was most telling among private institutions, while Asian Americans still held an advantage in gaining acceptance to the most selective public institutions. Acceptance rates in 1985 to public and private institutions classified by selectivity are shown in Table 1. However, in regions of rapid Asian population growth such as California, by 1985 chances for Asian applicants of being accepted by highly selective public institutions were already declining to below those of all other groups, as will be shown later.

This paper focuses on access to the most selective undergraduate institutions because diplomas from top institutions confer certain competitive advantages in American society. Asian

Table 1
Asian American Admission Rates to 4-Year Undergraduate
Institutions in 1985

Governance:	Public		Private	
Group:	Asian	Total	Asian	Total
Selectivity:				
Most Selective (50% or less accepted)	47%	38%	30%	34%
More Selective (51–80% accepted)	67%	68%	69%	68%
Less Selective (81–95% accepted)	81%	87%	82%	84%
Least Selective (>95% accepted)	98%	97%	88%	93%
All Responding Institutions	66%	72%	48%	62%
N institutions	167	328	338	689

Hunter M. Breland, Gita Wilder, and Nancy J. Robertson, *Demographics, Standards, and Equity: Challenges in College Admissions* (AACRAO, ACT, The College Board, Educational Testing Service, and NACAC, 1986).

American access to less select institutions is also below average, but consideration of that issue deserves separate treatment. One plausible explanation for lower Asian American admissions, absent affirmative action, would be that they are simply less well prepared for college work. Examination of empirical evidence does not support such a hypothesis.

Qualifications for Higher Education

Affirmative action laws and guidelines presume long term, debilitating effects of sexism and racism on the developed abilities and academic achievements of women and members of minority groups. Asian Americans, in general, have failed to conform to a deficit model. While there were educational, psychological, and opportunity costs associated with their academic progress, even immigrants and refugees with limited mastery of English were by no means at a total disadvantage in competing for slots with the majority. To be sure, specific groups of refugee youth such as Cambodians, Hmong, and Laotians have not fared as well because they arrived with little formal education and virtually no

English. Many of them must make their way alone, without families for emotional and economic support. These economically, linguistically, and educationally disadvantaged refugees should be considered apart from other Asian American youth and are not the focus of this paper.

In 1985, 30 percent of White 18-year-olds but almost 70 percent of Asian/Pacific Islander Americans were candidates for the SAT or achievement tests required for admission to many selective colleges. Asian/Pacific Islander Americans were thus far less select as a group. Pacific Islanders constitute a small fraction of the college-bound population. This paper makes reference to Asian Americans with the understanding that Pacific Islanders are sometimes included in aggregated statistics. About 27 percent of Asian American testtakers reported that their best language was not English, compared to less than 2 percent of White testtakers. The mean SAT verbal scores of Asian/Pacific American and White college-bound seniors were 404 and 449, respectively. Their mean SAT mathematics scores were 518 and 490, respectively. These performance profiles were in line with the 1985–1986 ACT English and mathematics scores of Asian American and White testtakers.

When Asian American SAT-takers were classified according to whether English was their best language, the considerable verbal disadvantage of newcomers became apparent. The median SAT verbal scores of "English is best language" Asian American and White testtakers were 434 and 444, respectively. The median SAT verbal score of Asian Americans whose best language is not English was only 272, which was about a standard deviation below the median scores of English-not-best-language Mexican American and Puerto Rican testtakers. Nevertheless, these same English-not-best-language Asian American students recorded the highest SAT mathematics scores of all, 522. Validity studies have shown that the SAT mathematics scores of Asian American candidates whose best language is not English were likely to be underestimates of their true developed quantitative reasoning abilities; these students have not yet mastered English well enough to deal with mathematical problems presented in words. The discrepancy between their verbal and quantitative abilities limited their choice of major fields and handicapped newcomers in college admissions. But once in college, they earn above average grades. Quantitative test scores are better predictors of future performance for recent immigrants and refugees.

Not only did typical college-bound Asian Americans perform

competently on tests of developed reasoning abilities and academic achievements but they also reported longer hours spent on
homework, more earned credits in academic subjects, particularly
mathematics and sciences; higher cumulative grade point averages, and higher ranks in class than all other student groups.
Asian Americans participated in Advanced Placement (AP) programs, which offer college credits and sophomore standing on
the basis of AP test scores, at more than double the rate of college-
bound seniors. They have also won more than their share of local
and national honors such as being named National Merit Scholarship Program finalists and winners, Presidential Scholars and
finalists, Westinghouse Science Talent Search finalists, and ARTS
(a performing arts scholarship program) finalists.

Access to Selective Institutions

Asian Americans apply to the most selective institutions their
academic qualifications warrant and their families can afford.
Asian families make substantial sacrifices for top college degrees.
More than eight out of ten first-generation Chinese, Japanese,
and Korean American parents questioned in a 1984 study responded that they would sell their only house for their children's
college education if necessary; nor would they expect future support in return. Fewer than three out of ten Anglo parents with
children in the same schools responded in the same way.

Asian American communities were therefore stunned by a
1983 report from the East Coast Asian Student Union (ECASU)
that described results of a survey conducted by Asian American
students at 25 selective undergraduate institutions. ECASU students reported that Asian American applications had begun to
skyrocket in the late 1970s, but numbers admitted had increased
very little. In addition, they found that the admitted Asian American students were mainly from middle- and upper-class suburban
backgrounds. The authors concluded: "Those from inner cities
and from economically disadvantaged backgrounds are being left
outside the entrance gates . . . These facts point to an alarming
barrier to those of [us] who are seeking higher education and
better lives, both for ourselves and for our families. The answer
lies behind the closed doors of the college admissions process."
Admissions records from top private institutions on both coasts
have since confirmed student concerns about differential access
in the 1980s. From Stanford in California to Harvard in Mas-

sachusetts, Asian American admit rates were lower than White rates, and dropping further each year.

The critical mass of Asian students on campus needed to alarm policymakers into taking steps to slow down Asian American admissions varied among institutions. Princeton matriculated 27 Asian American freshmen in 1977. By 1978, the Asian admit rate had fallen. Despite decelerating admit rates, the number of Asian American Princeton freshmen grew. By 1985, there were 99. The year that saw the Asian American admit rate fall below average was 1980 at Brown. The number of Asian American freshmen was 59 during the previous academic year. Steadily declining admit rates, and higher academic credentials demanded of those admitted, kept the total number of Asian American freshmen below 100 for five years. Harvard doubled its enrollment of Asian American freshmen between 1976 and 1977. More than 100 freshmen in 1977 were Asian American. Asian American admit rates fell thereafter. More stringent standards were reported for Asian American applicants. In 1982, the mean combined SAT score of Asian Americans admitted to Harvard was 112 score points higher than White students', even though mean combined scores of White and Asian American applicants in their respective pools were close. Stanford's Asian American enrollment dropped from 5.7 to 4.8 percent in 1977. Asian American freshmen approached and hovered around 100 from 1978 onwards. Between 1982 and 1985, Asian American admission rates ranged between 66 and 70 percent of White applicants'. There were 119 Asian American freshmen by 1985.

Quotas or Diversity

The pattern of Asian American admissions during the second decade of affirmative action suggested a series of yellow lights that signaled: Caution! Go slow! Typically, Asian American enrollments would remain constant for several years before a modest increase, and then level off again. The figures show that relatively modest increases in Asian students were sufficient to alarm decisionmakers at selective colleges. Private institutions that use "academics plus" criteria could then fine-tune admit rates without resorting to quotas, known by all to be illegal under Title VI of the Civil Rights Act of 1964 and the Equal Protection Clause of the Fifth Amendment.

Deans of Harvard, Yale, and Princeton have issued public

statements on Asian American admission policies. All categorically denied the use of quotas for limiting Asian American enrollment. Each cited the visible presence of Asian Americans on campus as proof of fairness in admissions, and explained lower Asian admit rates by the institutional need for building each class according to an overall framework to ensure diversity and balance. A typical statement was that of Yale's Dean of Undergraduate Admissions on the undergraduate admission "target" system. While Yale does not set "quotas" or "ceilings" on the number of students from an ethnic pool, the university does have a "target" or expected notion of distributions within each class. While the first goal of the Admissions Office was to select the best-qualified class, diversity was deemed scarcely less important.

The desire to obtain a diverse student body was found constitutional in the deciding opinion written by Supreme Court Justice Lewis F. Powell for the landmark case, *Regents of the University of California v. Bakke*, in 1978. Justice Powell singled out the selection process of Harvard College as an illuminating example of programs " . . . which take race into account in achieving the educational diversity valued by the First Amendment. . . ." Asian Americans were nearing 14 percent of Harvard's freshman class in 1987. In the interest of diversity, Harvard has supported an active and successful program to recruit disadvantaged students from inner city Asian ethnic enclaves. Withal, the admit rate of Asian Americans to Harvard College remained about 40 percent below White students' in 1987. Given that nine justices of a divided Supreme Court of the United States wrote six separate opinions on the Bakke case and supported the lower court's recognition of a private right of action, well informed Asian Americans are understandably reluctant to seek remedy via the courts.

Administrative avenues for seeking equity in access have yet to be exhausted. Asian Americans have requested clarification of admissions policies from a number of the most selective colleges. Institutions have been responsive to varying degrees. Some schools have undertaken self-examinations. Princeton and Stanford have released summaries of their university committee reports. Members of the Asian American Students Association (AASA) took the initiative at Brown with a report on Asian American admissions policies and practices that elicited prompt response from the administration. In 1984, a subcommittee on Asian American admission, appointed by Brown University's Committee on Admission and Financial Aid, confirmed the students' findings of bias in admissions policies and procedures. Based on subcommittee recommendations, Brown University reaffirmed its commitment to affirmative action for disadvantaged minorities and carried out specific admissions policy and procedural changes.

A subcommittee at Stanford analyzed Asian American admissions for the academic years 1984 and 1985, taking into consideration articulated criteria for admission that could validly result in different rates of admission for different subgroups. Although no implicit quotas or conscious discrimination could be identified, all factors considered failed to explain fully differences in admit rates between Asian American and White applicants. Examination of effects of preferential admissions for alumni legacies, faculty and staff offspring, athletes, and protected affirmative action categories; academic and nonacademic ratings of Asian Americans, and choice of major fields, separately and together, could not account for the limited number of Asian American freshmen. Unconscious bias in subjective ratings that resulted in lower overall evaluations of Asian American applicants could not be ruled out as a cause of lower Asian American admit rates. The 1985–1986 annual report of Stanford's Committee on Undergraduate Admissions and Financial Aids clarified its admissions policies, affirmed a policy of nondiscrimination against applicants of Asian American or any other ethnic extraction, and initiated procedures for annual review of Asian American admissions to ensure fairness.

Princeton's Faculty and Student Committees on Undergraduate Admission and Financial Aid cited essentially the same reasons as Brown, Harvard, Stanford, and Yale for explaining lower Asian American admit rates. The committee reported that Asian Americans who were admitted presented somewhat stronger academic qualifications than the average, but held that their typically lower nonacademic ratings were justified. Alumni legacies, faculty and staff offspring, athletes, and underrepresented minorities, which together represented 34 to 42 percent of the applicant pools of the years studied, were excluded from the analyses. The committee concluded that overall, Princeton's evaluations of Asian American applicants were fair.

Did the findings of internal studies influence subsequent admissions policies and practices? Admission figures that followed internal reports were telling. Admit rates of Asian American applicants to Brown rose for two years after release of the university committee report. Similarly, the Asian American admit rate at Stanford rose to 89 percent of the White rate for Fall 1986 following the study on admit rates. The number of Asian American freshmen doubled to more than 200. On the other hand, the Princeton committee had reported in 1985 that Asian American admit rates compared favorably with unaffiliated White admit rates. Subsequently, Asian American freshmen fell by 25 percent for Fall 1986. These events support the hypothesis that an institution's rationale for differential treatment of Asian American applicants did influence subsequent admissions policies, practices, and procedures, which in turn redefined the upper limits of Asian American freshmen.

Selective institutions will go on being inundated by qualified Asian American applicants. Each institution will still construct entering classes according to predetermined plans. All want ethnic and socioeconomic diversity, departmental balance, broad geographic distribution, and other desiderata: athletes, underrepresented females and minorities in engineering and physical sciences, musicians, artists, and potential donors. Admissions policies and procedures adopted by a single selective institution to shape its student body might seem rational and fair, given finite resources and a host of conflicting interests. However, when results were aggregated across many institutions, patterns emerged that signaled pervasive exclusion.

Berkeley and UCLA

Similar patterns of differential access have been recorded at two of the most selective public universities in California. Public institutions as a rule admit students by inflexible, unambiguous procedures, follow politically mandated standards, and use eligibility formulas based on composite academic criteria. In 1984, Asian Americans represented 3.1 percent of the nation's total higher education enrollment. They were 10.3 percent of California's higher education enrollment. Forty-four percent of all Asian American college and university students resided in California. A goal of maintaining proportional representation in California's higher education system would be very difficult, given demographic and educational realities.

To be eligible for admission to one of the eight undergraduate campuses of the University of California (UC), students must have completed a sequence of high school course requirements and rank in the top 12.5 percent of their graduating class on the basis of grade point averages and standardized test scores. In 1983, 26 percent of Asian American high school graduates were UC eligible, compared to 15.5 percent of Whites and smaller percentages among other minority groups.

Berkeley is the flagship campus of the UC system and first choice of Asian Americans, particularly students from the San Francisco Bay Area. Almost 7 percent of California's population is Asian, but Asian Americans comprise 40 percent of residents in San Francisco County. Beginning in 1981, Asian American admit rates fell below White and overall rates. Between 1982 and 1986, enrollments of the two largest Asian ethnic groups, Chinese and Japanese, fell while numbers of the smaller Asian ethnic groups rose slightly. Filipino Americans remained targets for affirmative action until 1986. By 1984, total numbers in the freshman class, as well as a relative proportion of Asian American freshmen, began to fall. From a 1983 high of 1,239 freshmen, Asian Americans had dropped to 875 by 1986.

Asian American faculty, students, and Bay Area leaders sought clarification of Berkeley's admissions policies. An Asian American Task Force on University Admissions conducted analyses of applicant and enrollment data provided by the university. The Task Force report, released in 1985, concluded that little publicized changes in admissions procedures, such as an unannounced SAT verbal cutoff score in addition to SAT total score requirements for applicants who were not underrepresented minorities, had excluded Asian Americans. Most adversely affected were recent refugees and immigrants. Low income, Education Opportunity Program applicants—candidates for affirmative action—were redirected to other UC campuses unless they were among the underrepresented minorities. Poor Asian newcomers were again disproportionately affected. Admission rates for all Asian American subgroups fell consistently at the bottom of all applicant groups.

The use of a standard academic index to admit Berkeley applicants has been curtailed. In 1985, 60 percent of entering freshmen were admitted by academic index. The proportion was reduced to 50 percent in 1986. A majority of Asian American students were admitted on academic merit alone. They were the least likely of all groups to be admitted by supplemental, subjective criteria for the limited number of openings that remained after special action admissions. The Task Force, with attention from the media, appeared to have had a positive influence on Asian American admissions. Despite a 1985 policy of smaller freshman classes, Asian American admit rates have approached White rates again. Berkeley's entering freshman class for Fall 1985 had no clear majority. Non-Hispanic White students, at 48 percent, became a plurality of the class. Asian Americans were 27 percent of the freshmen.

For Fall 1987, a decision to accept only 40 percent of freshmen by academic index further limited the number of places potentially available to Asian Americans. Of the remaining 60 percent, 30 percent were reserved for affirmative action and special action admissions, and the remaining places were assigned by academic plus criteria. Two other policy changes will also affect Asian Americans adversely: eliminating preference for students who live within commuting distance, and changing preference for applicants from traditional feeder schools in favor of graduates of rural high schools and schools that had sent few graduates to Berkeley in the past. Graduates of Bay Area feeder schools, such as scholastically demanding Lowell High School with 65 percent Asian students, would no longer be able to count on Berkeley.

White freshmen also became a plurality on the UCLA campus by 1986. A number of changes had been introduced to curb the decline in White enrollment. Asian Americans, the only racial minority group no longer protected by affirmative action, were adversely affected by these admissions policy changes. Between 1978 and 1984, Asian American applicants had almost doubled. The crossover year was 1982, when the Asian admit rate fell below the White rate. Poor, recent immigrants were again ill-served because they were excluded from the protected pool of Student Affirmative Action applicants. Asian American freshmen enrollments fell from a high of almost 20 percent in 1981 and 1982 to about 15 percent. Admissions policy and criteria changes announced in December 1986 will further limit Asian American access. UCLA eliminated altogether, from Fall 1987 on, the use of the academic selection index which had been the criterion for admitting half of each class in recent years. The new policy, adopted from selective private institutions, articulated UCLA's intention to rely exclusively on subjective ratings. The criteria for ratings included the quality and content of high school courses and the difficulty of the high school programs, which are verifiable and would not present serious problems for most Asian American applicants. However, new criteria also included extracurricular activities and the ability of the student to express his or her commitment to such activities in personal essays. The subjective ratings will undoubtedly act as unexpected hurdles for Asian immigrants and refugees.

What was the critical mass that started chains of reactions from Berkeley and UCLA? The number of new Asian American freshmen had exceeded 1,000 at both institutions before changes came about. Asian American freshmen were 20 percent of entering classes before their admit rates began to fall below White rates. Bound by public accountability and limited by inflexible, politically mandated admissions standards, state higher education systems have not been as free as private institutions to curb Asian American participation. However, any changes in public higher education policies could be implemented systemwide and would thus have far greater impact on Asian American students.

Post Affirmative Action: Access and Equity

Discriminatory treatment in order to limit the numbers of ethnic minorities is hardly new. White ethnic groups from Southern and Eastern Europe, Jews, and visible minorities have been denied admission to elite campuses in years past. Ivy League colleges justified Jewish quotas fifty-odd years ago with phrases that are used verbatim today to explain lower Asian American admissions. American Jews were of European stock, whereas Asian Americans are easily recognizable. Identification of Jewish applicants presented problems that required some ingenious subterfuges by administrators. A Jewish quota was not introduced by Harvard College until 1922, when enrollment had reached 21.5 percent. Jews were almost 40 percent of Columbia College in 1918 before the administration acknowledged "a Jewish problem." Yale Corporation voted to restrict the size of future classes in 1923 in order to limit "the alien and unwashed element in college. . . ." Jews dropped to 13 percent of the freshman class at Yale that fall and hovered in the vicinity of 10 percent until the early 1960s. Institutions are far more sophisticated today. Few problems of identification arise for Asian Americans. Selective institutions recognize a potential problem when their numbers exceed representative proportions. In the political and social climate of the 1980s, alerted decisionmakers initiate subtle, preventive measures in consonance with contemporary laws and mores.

Not all Asian American subgroups have been affected equally

by the end of affirmative action. Asian American women have fared better than men because they can still be counted as underrepresented females. Asian American women have been admitted to medical and engineering schools at the same or higher rates than White women. Asian American men, on the other hand, have been admitted at lower rates than White men, and those admitted have had to present better academic credentials than White men. In the past year or two, Asian American women have also been admitted at higher rates than men to MIT, Harvard, and Stanford. Why did it happen? We can only conjecture. Asian American women typically present strong qualifications for and interest in science, technology, and mathematics. These academic factors might have worked in their favor at institutions that were recruiting women. Asian American males are also particularly interested and well qualified in quantitative fields, but these factors have weighed against them in admissions. Valedictorian, varsity athlete, school officer, and successful entrepreneur Yat-pang Au was rejected by Berkeley in 1987. The official reason was that he planned a double engineering major. It is possible that nonacademic ratings of Asian American women have been consistently and reliably competitive with other female applicants, but Asian American men ranked lower than other male applicants. A plausible alternative hypothesis is that subjective ratings of similar ascriptive, stereotypic qualities were considered positive for Asian American women but negative for men.

Some schools keep track of the ethnic composition of Asian American students. Chinese and Japanese Americans now must make way for Korean, Vietnamese, East Indian, Filipino, Thai, and other Asians. Applicants from the newer Asian groups may hold a temporary advantage as contributors to institutional diversity. The preponderance of evidence suggests that competition for admission to selective institutions remained among Asian Americans themselves with foreign Asian nationals, and to a lesser degree, with White applicants unendowed with social connections or athletic prowess. Asian Americans are treated as separate pools from underrepresented minorities and white students with prerogative rights, and therefore constitute no threat to these groups.

Whether numeric affirmative action goals remained institutional hopes for the future or became ceilings for a particularly minority group seemed to be situationally determined. As long as their numbers did not exceed national representative proportions, Asian Americans remained subjects for affirmative action. Beyond the national percentage, Asian Americans were called "overrepresented" and subject to bias in admissions. Should proportional representation be according to national, state, or local population counts? Is any of these appropriate as the standard for rationing merit based educational opportunities? Population counts are constantly shifting targets. In the next 20 years, California will become the first state without an ethnic majority. Other states will soon follow. Group differences remain, not always in favor of White males, in motivation and qualifications for postsecondary education. For Asian Americans, equal opportunity in access rather than proportional representation would retain the spirit of affirmative action.

Future Implications and Recommendations

Affirmative action in higher education was initiated in order to dismantle discriminatory policies and processes. Once representation in accordance with population counts was attained, discrimination was deemed moribund. But continuing problems encountered by Asian Americans show that true equality will not be so simply defined or easily won. Future implications of differential access based on race must be thought through. But first some popular misconceptions should be dispelled.

Quotas are not at issue. Quotas were straw men set up so that institutional spokespersons could issue categorical denials. But what differentiates a quota from a "target," apart from semantics? Responsible Asian Americans do not allege conspiracies. Nevertheless, they are concerned about subtle biases, intentional or otherwise, in admissions. Policies, practices, and procedures adopted by selective institutions still lead to rejections for well qualified Asian American applicants in favor of White students who are no better.

Furthermore, affirmative action goals for underrepresented minorities are not jeopardized by Asian Americans. That often cited concern is another red herring. Minorities for affirmative action are placed in separate pools and treated independently from White and Asian American applicants. The most selective institutions compete vigorously for qualified underrepresented minority applicants. Most minority college applicants plan major

fields that attract relatively fewer Asian Americans. The same is
true of women. Federal and state agencies support affirmative
action programs in schools and colleges in order to recruit underrepresented minorities and women for science and technology.
Qualified affirmative action candidates for these fields retain a
substantial advantage in admissions. In science and technology,
competition for access is among Asian Americans and with White
males.

Asian Americans do not diminish diversity. On the contrary,
increasing variety among Asian Americans can contribute to campus diversity by the richness of their racial, national, ethnic, cultural, linguistic, religious, social, economic, political, and educational backgrounds and experiences.

What are the implications of biases, however subtle, against a
minority group that exceeded national proportional representation through merit based competition with the majority? For
Asian American students themselves, the issue remains denial of
their right to pursue excellence in higher education. Indifference
to current Asian American concerns could have far greater impact for society in the long run.

What messages are conveyed to underrepresented minorities
and women by the Asian American experience? "You will be allowed to go thus far, and no further! Proportional representation
will be the ceiling for vaulting aspirations, not individual effort
and merit." To the majority, particularly males or individuals with
institutional connections: "There is no need to do your best, because institutional prerogatives will protect you from challenging
competition."

There are costs to institutions as well. Suppose the top undergraduate program, college A, accepted 1 in 7 White applicants
but 1 in 12 Asian American applicants from pools that are essentially alike. Typical accepted Asian Americans needed 100 points
more on combined SAT scores; they also had to be in the 97th
rather than 94th percentile in their high school class. The 40
percent of Asian Americans who would have been admitted, had
they been White, then go to colleges B, C, D, or E, their backups.
These schools, too, manifested some bias in admitting Asian
Americans, and the rejected Asian Americans fall back to their
second or third choice college X, Y, Z, or AA. This trickle-down
effect could work through most of the 100 or so selective institutions that accept less than half their applicants. From college A to

college ZZZZ, each would have admitted Asian Americans who were a little better qualified than their White classmates. Asian Americans, like women, earn somewhat better grades in college than predicted. The net result would be that academic excellence at each institution becomes somewhat diminished, because admission by merit has been compromised. Further, the stereotype of "SuperAsian" would be reinforced at the most selected institutions by stricter standards used for selecting Asian American students.

Other societies have imposed barriers to higher education for certain minority groups. What were the results? Malaysia promulgated policies that favor ethnic Malays over Indian and Chinese Malays. Top universities in the Soviet Union gave covert preference to Russians over other ethnic groups and Jews. Higher education policies with ethnic preferences have been studied in China, Indonesia, India, and Sri Lanka. Typical lack of candor in such preferential treatment invariably led to resentment. . . .

Imposing arbitrary numbers or proportions to limit access is not only misuse of affirmative action goals but also runs counter to the national interest. At a time when educators are deeply concerned about the "rising tide" of mediocrity among American youth, Asian Americans are being punished for their academic zeal. They are denigrated and excluded from selective programs for interest in and talent for science and technology, when our nation must accelerate research and development in order to compete economically in world markets increasingly dominated by Pacific Rim nations.

Beyond affirmative action, what is right? Middle class, Asian Americans should be evaluated as individuals by the same standards as the majority, with appropriate sensitivity for cultural differences. Disadvantaged, language minority Asian newcomers, on the other hand, deserve to be considered for admissions by criteria used for other disadvantaged, limited-English-proficient applicants. Section 601 of the Civil Rights Act was explicit: "No person in the United States shall, on the ground of race, color or national origin be excluded from participation in, be denied the benefits of or be subjected to discrimination under any program or activity receiving Federal financial assistance." We need to remind ourselves of the breadth and vision of that law.

THE BERKELEY SQUEEZE[2]

For almost the past two decades universities have tried to redress discrimination by setting different admissions standards for
different ethnic groups. Few top-ranking schools worked harder
at affirmative action than the University of California, Berkeley.
But though Berkeley largely succeeded in creating racial "balance" where other universities failed, the result hasn't made anyone happy. Just about every ethnic group on Berkeley's campus is
now up in arms.

The loudest complaints have been those by Asian Americans,
who made up one-quarter of last year's incoming freshmen. In
charges picked up widely by news media, they claim that discrimination is keeping their number artificially low. For Berkeley's
blacks, getting in isn't the problem. It's graduating that's tough.
Affirmative action has brought more blacks on campus, but less
than one-third of them end up getting a Berkeley diploma. The
rest quit school or transfer, blaming racism and an administration
that seems to care more about packing them in than helping them
out. Hispanics share the same frustrations. Less than half of them
leave with degrees. Last but not least—not yet, anyway—come
the whites. Their share of new freshmen dropped from 58 percent in 1982 to 39 percent in 1987—well below their share of the
population.

Racial realignment has brought racial tension. The raw evidence ranges from the "Nips go home" graffiti in the bathrooms
of Evans Hall (the main math and science building) to attacks on
black students and the trashing of the offices of the African Students Association.

Berkeley's old admissions methods and the legislative guidelines behind them, fuzzy but well-meaning, were devised when
California's colleges and universities had a lot of whites, not
enough blacks and Hispanics, and hardly any Asians. "It's something everyone's going to face sooner or later," said Berkeley Vice
Chancellor Roderic Park. "We're just there first."

Berkeley is there first for several reasons. When California's
Asian population—heavily concentrated in the Bay area—began

[2]Reprint of an article by James S. Gibney. *New Republic* 198:15–17, April 11,
1988. Reprinted with permission.

to soar during the late '70s, so did the number of Asian applicants to Berkeley. From 1979 to 1984 applications by Asians rose at an average *annual* rate of 21 percent. At the same time, a rapid increase in the state's Hispanic population caused Berkeley to boost its affirmative action intake of Hispanics. Their proportion among entering freshmen jumped from 6.1 percent in 1981 to 17.1 percent in 1987. Finally, the steady inflation of private university fees made the U.C.'s already low in-state tuition ($1,500 a year) look better to everyone. In 1974 Berkeley could admit all applicants who had the necessary minimum academic qualifications. Thirteen years later it could let in less than half of all applicants whose grades and test scores made them "eligible." Roughly one-fifth of those turned away had near-perfect 4.0 grade point averages.

Asian Americans are high-stakes players in Berkeley's new numbers game. Asian American high school graduates have a higher U.C.-eligibility rate (26 percent) than whites (16 percent), Hispanics (six percent), or blacks (four percent). A greater proportion of those eligible graduates apply to the U.C. system. And no U.C. campus is more popular among Asians than Berkeley. In 1987, for example, it drew 5,200 applications from the 7,000 Asian Americans who were U.C. eligible.

The Asian American community was upset in 1984 when it noticed a 21 percent drop in newly enrolled Asians from the previous year. Led by Judge Ken Kawaichi of the Alameda Superior Court and Judge Lillian K. Sing of the San Francisco Municipal Court, the newly formed Asian American Task Force on University Admissions came out with a report that accused Berkeley of discriminating against Asians. The ensuing controversy sent both the university and the Asian American community into a bean-counting frenzy.

Behind the 1984 plunge were changes in Berkeley's admission policies. Specifically, the university decided not to include whites and Asians in its Educational Opportunity Program (EOP). Previously EOP had guaranteed admission to eligible students if they were economically disadvantaged (family income under $20,000) and their parents were not college educated. That year, however, Berkeley attracted more EOP applicants than it could handle. So Asian and white EOP applicants were thrown in with the regular admission pool. Since there were more Asian than white EOP students, more Asians were rejected.

In 1985 Berkeley added what Asian Americans considered

insult to injury by adopting a set of "supplemental" admissions criteria. Forty percent of incoming freshmen are now selected solely on the basis of grades and standardized test results. Asians and whites are admitted to this group at equal rates. Another 38 percent of incoming freshmen are automatically offered spots under affirmative action or "special action" (recruited athletes, disabled students, etc.). That leaves 22 percent—mostly whites and Asians—who are judged on their grades and scores plus supplemental criteria that include a written essay, extracurricular activity, English composition skills, and foreign language capability.

The administration says it uses these criteria to make better choices among candidates who are statistically almost identical. Asian Americans don't see things that way. Newly arrived Asian immigrants, they say, are too busy learning English to study what the College Entrance Examination Board considers "foreign" languages: French, German, Latin, Hebrew, or Spanish. To them, the new criteria look more like a new way to weed out Asian applicants.

Did Berkeley consciously discriminate against Asians in making these changes? The Department of Justice is still mulling whether to launch a formal investigation. But some of the evidence doesn't look good. The 1984 EOP decision should have gone through Berkeley's Academic Senate. Instead, it came from within the administration. Now no one in California Hall can remember who made the decision. Also mysterious was a proposed "floor" of 400 on SAT verbal scores—a measure that would have hurt the many Asian American applicants who speak English as a second language. First university officials told Judge Kawaichi that it didn't exist. Then they said that it existed but was never implemented. As for the supplemental admissions criteria, Assistant Vice Chancellor Bud Travers admits that the foreign language provision needs fixing. But he insists that, in general, the statistics show the criteria affecting whites and Asians equally. Asians have their doubts. Since the university controls the admissions figures, looking at the numbers is like playing three card monte on the sidewalks of New York. Even with both eyes on the action the cards are hard to follow.

Chancellor Ira Michael Heyman has soothed Asian feelings by appointing Asians to several committees now reviewing admissions. "We're not asking for any special treatment for Asians," says

Kawaichi. "We're asking for fair treatment for everybody." What Kawaichi and other Asian Americans consider "fair" is an admission system that relies on grades and test scores. Judging applicants by essays and extracurricular activities is culturally suspect. Many Asian American families, the argument goes, regard something like a role in a school play as a frivolous distraction from the hours of study they feel are needed to get ahead. Kawaichi also believes that it's almost impossible to assign objective worth to subjective criteria like essays: His solution: "We know what grades measure."

But an "A" from Lowell High in well-to-do San Francisco is not the same as an "A" from Castlemont High in down-and-out Oakland. Moreover, if high school washouts like Albert Einstein were to apply to Berkeley, the objective criteria favored by many Asian Americans would keep them out. They would also exclude most black and Hispanic applicants. Asians and blacks don't like to talk about that. Activists on both sides are in what William Banks, a black professor of Afro-American studies on the vice chancellor's staff, calls "political alignment." Asian Americans support affirmative action, and blacks support them in their struggle against discrimination. Whatever the rank and file may think, leaders from both groups won't admit that admissions is a zero-sum game. Whether Asians like it or not, an admissions system capable of handling a wide variety of socioeconomic and ethnic groups—and of attracting bright, well-rounded students—must be broad to be fair. That means using more than just grades and test scores.

For now, black and Hispanic applicants remain protected by affirmative action. In keeping with a 1974 resolution by the California State Legislature, the University of California has tried to create a student body that reflects the ethnic composition of California's high school graduates. Blacks, Hispanics, and other groups traditionally "underrepresented" at Berkeley are let in if they have the minimum necessary academic qualifications. But the resolution makes no provision for the presence of a minority of overachievers—the Asian Americans. Asians, with eight percent of the state's high school graduates, now have 26 percent of the places in Berkeley's freshman class. Meanwhile whites, with 62 percent of high school graduates, have only 39 percent of the freshman class. The combination of Asian achievement and affirmative action for other groups has led to the white majority being disproportionately underrepresented.

The imbalance is going to get worse before it gets better. California's Hispanic and Asian populations will continue to grow well past the year 2000. The result: more regular Asian applicants and more protected places set aside for Hispanics. Blacks face a different prospect. Under the current affirmative action plan, they will remain protected for at least five years after attaining "parity" with their proportion among high school graduates. Blacks at Berkeley are now over parity. Despite a significant improvement in their grades and test scores, they won't be ready by 1992 to compete under regular admissions. Although California's white population will dwindle, the drop won't be enough to accommodate the increase in Asians and Hispanics. So far the whites have reacted to their reduced numbers without making much noise. But sooner or later some litigious white folks are going to start wondering why their Jane or Johnny didn't get in.

One solution to this mess is simple. Drop protection of applicants on the basis of race. Another alternative would be to award underrepresented applicants points toward regular admission. Or to link the concept of ethnic representation not to the proportion of all high school graduates, but to the proportion of those who are U.C. eligible. One thing is clear: letting blacks and Hispanics in by the front door so they can drop out the back does nobody any good. If the current black graduation rate remains constant, more blacks will fail to get a diploma in the next three years than the number who earned degrees in the last decade.

At a recent hearing on the charges made by Asian Americans, black Assemblywoman Teresa Hughes—sponsor of the 1974 regulations—reacted by denouncing the University of California for discriminating against *all* minorities. That charge avoids the central conundrum, as do all the proposed solutions. If Asians are underrepresented based on their grades and test scores, it is largely because of affirmative action for other minority groups. And if blacks and Hispanics are underrepresented based on their fraction of the population, it is increasingly because of the statistical overachievement of Asians. Both complaints can't be just, and the blame can no longer be placed solely on favoritism toward whites.

LATINO FACULTY AT THE BORDER[3]

I am regularly asked why Latinos do not fare better in school and society, usually by well-meaning colleagues who are genuinely troubled by the problem. Having spent eight years in the Catholic seminary studying for the priesthood, I tend to be an optimist and put the best gloss on any problem. So, for all the years I've been writing about the education of Latinos, I have always taken the high road: I have variously "relied upon the reservoir of goodwill in the majority," counted upon colleagues to "follow their own institutional self-interest in seeking and graduating Hispanic students," and encouraged need-based aid programs because "in any need-based aid program, Latinos, who constitute one of the most impoverished communities, will more likely participate." I have delivered dozens of lectures (usually during Hispanic Awareness Weeks or Cinco de Mayo celebrations) exhorting my people to do well and encouraging institutional leaders to help my people.

But, like the Reverend Leon Sullivan's finally giving up on White South Africans, I have come to believe, reluctantly, that the majority of persons in higher education do not think a problem exists, do not act as if a problem exists, or do not care about minority achievement. I say this, knowing how sharply critical and pessimistic this will seem to readers. However, I believe Anglo racism is at the heart of the problem. Even the self-help I have urged and the patronage of a small number of majority colleagues cannot resolve the clear and long-standing legacy of historical racism toward Latino populations in the United States.

For this proposition I could cite historical evidence, from the annexation of the southwestern United States to the colonization of Puerto Rico, to the Bracero Program and "Operation Wetback," to the English-only movement and long-standing immigration practices; I could cite more subtle practices, such as the heightened reliance on standardized testing and the indifference

[3]Article by Michael A. Olivas, professor of law, University of Houston. *Change* Magazine 20:6–9, My/Je '88. Reprinted with permission of the Helen Dwight Reid Educational Foundation. Published by Heldref Publications, 4000 Albemarle St., N.W., Washington, D.C. 20016. Copyright © 1988.

of philanthropy to Hispanic communities. This laundry list could continue but advances no purpose. Instead, I choose one issue on which to focus my point: the need for more Latino professors. I believe that this need is the single most important key to any hope for increasing Latino access.

While the need may be self-evident to *Change* readers and intuited by many educators, the extraordinary extent of the problem is not widely known, or is misunderstood. According to the most recent Office for Civil Rights figures (lamentably inadequate as they are), Hispanics constitute 1.5 percent of all faculty and just 1.1 percent of all tenured faculty.

As paltry as these figures are, they mask an even more startling under-representation, for the numbers include *all* fields of the professoriate and report *all* Hispanics, even some who would be surprised to find themselves carried on their colleges' books as minority faculty. I have found institutions that pad their figures shamelessly and that list retired, resigned, and temporary faculty as if they were active participants in institutional life. After teaching one special course as an adjunct on an extension campus for a university, I found myself listed seven years later in the institution's catalogue (one law school lists a 70-year-old emeritus a decade later). Such examples are legion and probably double the true number of Hispanic faculty. Professors from Spain, Brazil, Portugal, and South America are routinely identified and misleadingly tallied as "minority" faculty. In several universities, Anglo women married to Latinos have been counted.

While I do not have the space here to dissect racial enumeration practices, suffice it to say that institutions employ far too few Latino faculty, employ far too many statistical tricks in their reporting, and that both practices evidence bad faith.

Although all fields are under-represented, I am going to use law faculty as an example, both because I know the practices in it better than in other fields, and because law professors have an influence in higher education beyond their small numbers. However, the problems Latinos face in entering the teaching of law mirror the problems of minorities in the academy at large: exceedingly small numbers, arbitrarily employed hiring criteria, and sheer prejudice. With adjustments for different trade usages and academic customs, the case I now recite resembles that in most disciplines.

First, one starts with exceedingly small numbers: fewer than three dozen of the 5,700 law teachers (two-thirds of 1 percent) in the approximately 180 accredited law schools in the fifty states and the District of Columbia are Latinos; of these 35, there are 20 Mexican-Americans, 5 Puerto Ricans, and the remainder are Cuban or of other Hispanic origin.

Although law faculty positions are not as plentiful now as when law enrollments were soaring, a substantial number of vacancies are filled each year. In 1986–87, the most recent year for which data are available, 570 law professors (10 percent of the total) entered teaching. In that year, only *one* new Latino entered law teaching in the nation, and two left . . . if it is possible to lose ground, under the circumstances, we lost ground last year. Because several schools have more than one Latino teaching law, the 35 are concentrated in 24 schools (the University of New Mexico has 5 Latinos on its law faculty, earning it a designation as a nuclear-free zone or historical landmark). A recent study by the Society of American Law Teachers (SALT) found that 30 percent of respondent law schools had *no* minority faculty, either Latino or black, while another 34 percent had only one minority teacher. (Even if one includes black and Puerto Rican law schools, only 7 percent of the law professoriate is minority.)

These extraordinary data show the small extent to which minorities, especially Mexican-Americans and Puerto Ricans, have entered the legal academy. Of course, these data are similar to other fields, from the least to the most prestigious. Data gathered by National Chicano Council on Higher Education officials reveal there are only three Chicano professors of higher education, seven physicists, a dozen in chemistry, with slightly greater numbers in sociology, psychology, and bilingual education. By any measure, these numbers are appalling.

These figures constitute the demand side. What about the supply side? In 1986–87, all minority law students constituted 10.6 percent of law enrollments. Of these, 1,512 were Chicanos (1.3 percent), the same percentage of law enrollments as in 1975–76, when 1,443 Mexican-Americans were enrolled. To be sure, there are relatively few Latinos in the law-school "pipeline," but the metaphor is misleading. First, the consumers (law schools) are also the producers; why don't they see their responsibility to recruit and graduate more Latino lawyers? Second, even 1,400 graduates a year produce a very large pool of eligible Latinos over time, certainly sufficient to produce more than the *one* Mexican-American lawyer hired to teach in 1986–87.

What went wrong? What can be done? Is law teaching the

pantheon, with law-review membership and Supreme Court clerkships the essential requirements for entry, and we're simply not qualified?

Hardly. Considerable data have been gathered on last year's new teachers, and their quality is indeed high. Nonetheless, of the 577 new law teachers hired, only 38 percent had law review experience (versus 48 percent of the total professoriate); 16 percent had been elected to Coif membership (the national honorary reserved for the top 10 percent of graduates); 10 percent held the L.L.M., an advanced graduate degree in law (versus 23 percent of the total); and only 14 percent had ever published an article or legal writing. Most interestingly, one-third had no legal experience before they entered teaching; 30 percent had not even passed a bar exam. It was not minority teachers who pulled down these data; the minorities who were hired statistically resemble their majority counterparts.

What is operating here? A powerful mythology permeates law hiring, as it does hiring in nearly all academic fields—that there are too few minority candidates for too few positions, and they possess unexceptional credentials for the highly credentialed demand. I believe these data paint the opposite picture—that, for most schools, white candidates with good (but not sterling) credentials are routinely considered and hired, while the high-demand/low-supply mythology about minorities persists.

As I have alleged, not only does this myth not square with available data, but the practices ignore the supply-side responsibility of law schools and the lack of marketplace alternatives for Latinos in other legal employment. After all, major firms and governments are not much more accessible to Latinos than are law faculties. The answer is an unpopular one because it entails racism, which permeates the academy as it does all of society.

That this is so should not surprise us, as higher education reflects our society, draws from it, and collaborates with it. After all, the legal road to *Brown v. Board of Education* was a series of higher education cases, suits in our lifetime that assaulted a segregated citadel. The poisonous residue of those practices remains. Many of today's senior faculty directly benefited from having it all to themselves, from not having to compete—in school or the academic marketplace—with women or minorities. To a large extent, they still don't compete, particularly not with Latinos.

After all my cynicism, what can be done? My suggestions are

aimed at law teaching, but they apply to many professions and fields of study.

As in many professions, there is a formal hiring fair, or "meat market," for law hiring, one that inadequately reaches or serves Latino applicants—the conference of the American Association of Law Schools (AALS). Law schools could make that meeting a far more effective device for recruiting minorities. Recent minority alumni could be encouraged to register for the conference, and the forms could be sent to recent graduates who express an interest. I regularly carry AALS forms to conferences, scouting out minority talent; I send out dozens of forms each year, encouraging minority attorneys to consider teaching. Others could do this, thereby widening the formal stream of applicants.

Similarly, faculty could keep in touch with recent graduates who are undertaking advanced legal studies, making legal presentations, clerking, and engaging in private or government practice. Law deans should identify minority practitioners who may not wish to leave their firm but who might be persuaded to teach as an adjunct, judge a moot court, or lecture on their field of expertise in a lunch forum, continuing legal education seminar, or other teaching situation. This would expose students to minority professionals and encourage minority attorneys to consider teaching as a possible alternative career opportunity.

Many full-time teachers began teaching as adjunct or part-time faculty. Every legal writing program staffed by local attorneys or senior law students should be required to include minorities on its teaching staff. Faculty in all disciplines should encourage promising minority students by hiring them as research assistants or teaching assistants, to mentor them, inculcate scholarly values, and ensure a fuller stream of persons who will aspire to eventual careers in teaching. Schools should always "be on the prowl" for promising prospects, especially minority prospects.

Schools could structure interviews so that minorities can succeed, and can increase the likelihood of minorities' succeeding by interviewing several minority candidates and by hiring more than one. One of the first law schools to hire Chicano faculty hired two at once in the early 1970s. That school (New Mexico) now has five Latino and a total of seven minority faculty members. It is clear that much more effort needs to be made to increase the critical mass of minority teachers in individual schools (remember: only a third of all law schools have two or more minorities). Minority faculty should be appointed to chair search committees, not merely serve as the lone member charged with affirmative-action responsibilities.

A combination of formal and informal methods must be used to identify faculty. As with recruiting graceful seven-footers, strong-armed quarterbacks, or musical prodigies, recruitment requires diligent looking. Historically black law schools and Puerto Rican institutions have always been able to recruit lawyers, yet few majority schools recruit faculty or graduates from them. Minority legal organizations have contributed many extraordinarily talented attorneys to the teaching ranks and regularly attract excellent minority law graduates. Government service has recruited a disproportionate array of minority attorneys because of less elite hiring criteria, more perceived openness to minorities, and few opportunities at elite law firms—which tend to have very few minority partners or associates. Indeed, faculty enter legal teaching from a variety of backgrounds; in this regard, law schools have a larger stream of candidates than do other academic fields, which recruit new faculty directly from doctoral programs. However, almost no field is without minority candidates. I believe it is a self-serving mythology that minority candidates are "flooded with offers" when every year, qualified and interested minorities are looking for academic work but do not find it.

One way for a university to encourage the recruitment of minority faculty is to provide an additional "slot," or position, reserved for the minority teacher. Most universities have funding mechanisms that reserve resources for the occasional superstar, faculty spouse, senior administrator, or other out-of-the-ordinary hiring; let resources be reserved that same way for minority hiring. To turn up the heat, insist that schools or departments with one or no minority faculty members cannot hire any majorities until they achieve success in attracting minorities. Only courageous provosts, deans, and presidents can effect this practice, but courage is what we need.

One more idea: placement and search firms are regularly used by major law firms and by universities in administrative searches; they could be used by law schools and other departments to find the minority faculty talent we so desperately need.

The several ideas suggested here are not revolutionary or even that unusual. Most law schools employ them, or versions of them, when looking for hard-to-find specialists; every law faculty has had to search for a specialized tax or bankruptcy or decedents-estates teacher, all of whom have been less readily available than, say, a contracts or torts teacher. The same diligence should be used in looking for minority law teachers.

I am convinced that there is a good supply of Latinos in most fields who are interested in and qualified for teaching. This is more a demand-side issue, and institutions should take more seriously their obligation to demand more minority faculty.

It is little wonder that Latinos have not fared well in the academy. The condition of Hispanic education is appalling. Even spending more money has not drastically improved matters, since majority decision makers and educators simply do not appear to be concerned. The best concern that could be shown is to hire more Latino teachers, in all disciplines, and to make it a priority to produce more teachers. Teachers and scholars make a difference in their instruction, their writing, their service, and their characterization of social issues. They serve as useful irritants, interpreters of society, and as role models for their students.

I have chosen to critique law professor hiring practices, but any field could be similarly analyzed. The lamest excuses exist in the social and behavioral sciences, to which many Latino scholars have been drawn. Many minority faculty work in minority institutions or low-prestige colleges, which then removes them from consideration in more prestigious schools. One of the most distinguished Chicano historians labors at a state teachers college, with a teaching load of four courses per semester. This pattern is extremely common. Given the proper support and opportunities, many more minority faculty members could successfully perform at research institutions. In an earlier book (*The Dilemma of Access*), I found startling evidence that minority faculty were not even reasonably represented in the least prestigious sector—community colleges—where few faculty hold the doctorate or engage in research.

In an eloquent law review essay, law professor Rachel Moran described the phenomenon of being "a society of one":

The psychological and social consequences of membership in a Society of One are pervasive and severe. The lone minority or woman professor is likely to encounter two extreme reactions. Some students and faculty will expect the minority or woman professor to serve as a representative of all minorities and women. These expectations will manifest themselves in demands for compliance with an impossible standard of performance. Another group will stigmatize the isolated minority or woman professor by assuming that he or she is inherently less capable than white male colleagues and was only appointed because of affirmative action. These dehumanizing views ignore the unique individual characteristics of minority and women law professors by either elevating them to superhuman symbol or reducing them to substandard political appointment. Both reactions have devastating consequences. An impossible standard of performance is a sure-fire formula for disappointment and failure. A negative expectation about academic promise may become a self-fulfilling prophecy. . . . A lone minority or woman law professor cannot discount the salience of race, ethnicity, and gender in the legal academy. Yet, in standing apart as a Society of One, these professors cannot assume the limited diversity on law faculties implies equality or even a grudging respect.

To be sure, many faculty of all stripes will find their work alienating, solitary, or unsatisfactory. I believe, however, that minority faculty are made to feel more isolated than are their majority colleagues and that isolation leads to disaffection and attrition. My discussions with disaffected Latino academics, both former law faculty and those in other disciplines, lead me to conclude that many of these instances could have been avoided with better support and reduced tension. Most encountered the "Society of One" syndrome and felt that they had regularly encountered hostile colleagues or racist students. While some feel relieved to be away from their situation, many feel bitterly betrayed that their original choice of careers was curtailed by prejudice. This attrition, like Latino attrition generally, seems an extraordinary waste in light of dire needs.

As a Chicano law professor, I fully appreciate the extent to which I and Latino colleagues have greater responsibilities; our service contributions and informal duties at times seem overwhelming. However, unless higher education takes more seriously *its* responsibilities to seek out others like us, and to behave differently toward Latinos, the extraordinary cycle of exclusion from faculty ranks will continue. Higher education is poorer for *its* loss.

VOTING WITH HIS FEET[4]

In a protest that was as alarming as it was original, Harvard Law School professor Derrick Bell last week declared not a sit-in but a walkout: he announced that he would take a leave of absence at the end of this academic year and would return to work only when Harvard added a tenured "woman of color" to the law faculty. "I cannot continue to urge students to take risks for what they believe," he said, "if I do not practice my own precepts." Added Bell, whose salary is about $100,000 a year: "I will view removing myself from the payroll as a sacrificial financial fast." His action won praise from colleagues all over the country, though no one else chose to follow suit.

The immediate cause of Bell's decision was Harvard's refusal to consider tenure for visiting professor Regina Austin, a black woman on the law faculty at the University of Pennsylvania. In rejecting Austin's candidacy, Harvard cited a three-year-old rule prohibiting tenure offers to visiting professors. But that technicality did not blunt Bell's anger at the school's hiring policies, which he once characterized as an attempt to recruit people "who look black and think white." Bell, who is black, now concedes that the description was "a bit unfair." But he still sees a "gap between the school's saying 'We're trying as hard as we can for diversity' and the hiring record." That record fully supports Bell's complaint: despite the administration's attempts to increase minority representation, the law-school staff of 60 tenured faculty boasts only three blacks (all men) and five women.

The key obstacle in many disciplines, according to various studies, is not simply racial or gender discrimination but also a scarcity of qualified candidates. Of 3,553 doctorates offered in the humanities in 1988, for example, 2,791 went to whites, and only 110 to blacks, 138 to Hispanics, and 197 to Asians. Last year the Washington-based National Research Council reported that of 13,158 Ph.D.s awarded in the sciences, only 275 went to blacks. Although black university enrollment has increased slightly in the past year, chances for substantial improvement are hardly promising.

The paucity of talent, meanwhile, has led to an unseemly

[4]Reprint of an article by *Time* magazine staff writer. Copyright 1990 The Time Inc. Magazine Company. Reprinted with permission.

bounty hunt, with big-budget schools scrambling to offer huge salaries and perks for highly qualified minority candidates. The State University of New York recently lured black African-studies expert Ali Mazrui from the University of Michigan with a seductive phone call from Governor Mario Cuomo and a salary of $105,000.

Bell has been inundated with offers from other schools since his announcement but has no plans to move. With all its shortcomings, he says, "Harvard is actually ahead of many other places."

EXCLUSIVE OPPORTUNITIES[5]

In the early 1970s, J. Stanley Pottinger, then director of the Office of Civil Rights in the Department of Health, Education, and Welfare, spent much of his time explaining what the emerging new program of affirmative action would *not* mean for higher education. For example, it would not mean minority quotas in faculty hiring. Any numerical requirement used to "favor any group," he said, was by definition "a restrictive ceiling or quota for all others."

Nor was reverse discrimination justified as a way of compensating for past discrimination against women and minorities. What was required, Pottinger said, was "adherence to fair procedures," which meant a "good faith effort" on the part of colleges and universities to open up faculty opportunities to everyone so that they could begin "to deal with the problems of exclusion and discrimination."

Bernice Sandler, director of the Project on the Status and Education of Women and a vigorous advocate of affirmative action, made clear why blacks should not be hired simply because they are blacks or women because they are women. "No institution is required to hire women or minorities on the basis of sexual or racial preference," she said. "To do so would be clearly illegal. Affirmative action is not aimed at creating preference but at ending preference for white males which has always existed in academia."

[5]Reprint of an article by John H. Bunzel, senior research fellow, Hoover Institution. *American Enterprise* 1:47–51, March/April 1990.

Left to their own devices, universities had not shown a marked interest in actively recruiting women and minorities for faculty positions. Affirmative action was promoted as a remedy aimed at removing the many barriers so that women and minorities could have an equal chance at all the good jobs so long denied them. But what initially was viewed as an attempt to prevent the perpetuation of past inequities would soon be directed to different purposes. Efforts by the academic world to open up faculty opportunities to everyone, to recruit faculty candidates broadly, to make sure that the evaluation of a person's qualifications and performance was not "racially infected"—these sound principles have been gradually transformed. Today, on many campuses, "treating equally" has increasingly been subordinated to a "special treatment" policy that considers race itself the predominant— sometimes exclusive—factor in faculty hiring, thereby eliminating other arbitrarily defined candidates from equal consideration.

At San Francisco State University, the quota mentality has insinuated itself into faculty recruitment. In keeping with the president's "firm stand on affirmative-action hiring," the affirmative-action coordinator has stressed the need for "a faculty that proportionately represents the ethnic diversity of this campus and the greater community [of San Francisco]." Deans have been told by the provost that "no search is exempt from this affirmative-action effort." In 1984, the provost sent a memo approving the English Department's request for two new faculty appointments, "but with the stipulation that the candidates recommended to me be nonwhite. Let me underscore that the stipulation is an absolute condition." In 1988, a dean received written approval for two new faculty positions in his school "for the purposes of affirmative-action minority hiring only." As one senior faculty member said, "The hypocrisy of it all is that the administration regularly denies that their affirmative-action hiring policy is an exclusionary one in practice. What happens is that all candidates who are interested in an advertised faculty position are invited to apply—after all, the law says you cannot discriminate against anyone on the basis of race or sex or background. But once all applications are in, the white candidates are simply removed from consideration. The shame of it is they never knew they never had a chance."

Consider how an affirmative-action search was conducted in a large department at San Francisco State. At its first meeting, reports a member of the hiring committee, the chairperson in-

structed the committee "to save time and energy by not examining any applications from white males. And so any number of
excellent applications—some were from men studying overseas
on Fulbright grants—went into the wastebasket. If we could not
tell for sure that the applicants were minority, phone calls were
made to references to be certain they were." One male with an
Indian-sounding name and wide experience teaching on several
reservations was interviewed. His scholastic record was outstanding, as was his mastery of Indian languages and history. "At the
interview," the committee member says, "the questioning was
done mostly by an Indian woman. After he left the room, she said
that he was the best candidate she had ever met. He was never
considered, however. Although he had made Indian studies one
of his specialties, he was ruled ineligible because he was white."

In March 1989, the faculty hiring committee in another department wrote a memo with its recommendations of well-
qualified candidates who were designated as "hireable." Its first
four choices for the full department to consider were minorities
or "persons of color," as were the next two candidates, listed separately, all of whom were "well qualified and hireable." Then followed the names of six additional candidates—all of them
white—who the committee said were "also well qualified but not
hireable"—not hireable because, by the terms established earlier,
white candidates were automatically excluded.

A former department chairman remembers a search for a new
faculty member that took a special turn to prevent the department from having to hire someone who was not among the top
candidates. "We could have invited a young black woman with
much weaker academic credentials to come to the campus for an
interview," he said. "But we knew how affirmative action worked.
If we had brought her here, we would have had to send her name
forward to the dean along with those of two white women who
everyone on the committee agreed were unquestionably better
qualified. We knew in advance that only the black woman would
have been approved by the dean. . . . And so she was not invited
to the campus," he said. "To put her on the list was automatically to disqualify the others. To leave her off the list was the only
way to give either of the two white women a chance to get the
dean's approval."

Affirmative-action hiring has been put into practice in different ways. Sometimes it merely confirms the current academic
wisdom in many quarters that white males cannot possibly teach

certain courses even if they have been appropriately trained. Last
winter, a white male with a Ph.D. in the social sciences inquired in
person about openings in Stanford University's new Culture,
Ideas, and Values course that has replaced the Western Culture
freshman requirement. He was told, simply and directly, "Only
racial minorities will be hired to fill the slots in the Europe and
Americas 'track'." At California State University, San Bernardino,
a white Ph.D. who has held both part-time and full-time lecturer
positions in sociology and criminal justice for eight years was
informed by a campus administrator that, as he relates it, "I
would never be considered for a tenure-track position because of
'affirmative-action considerations'."

Nor is this form of exclusion reserved only for white males. At
California State University, Humboldt, a white woman with a
Ph.D. (who had been teaching courses there on a yearly basis
since 1983) applied for a temporary lecturer position in her field.
In addition to classroom experience, she had written a book and
articles in professional journals. But none of that mattered. A
black woman applied, at which point the administration immediately changed the temporary slot into a full-time tenure-track
position that could be used by the department only if she took it.
When the black candidate turned it down, the administration
took back the full-time position. The white woman was ineligible
for the full-time job because she was the wrong color.

A major question raised by recruitment procedures is which
job advertisements written to attract minority candidates are legally permissible. At Ohio Wesleyan University, an advertisement
was placed in the major journal in this particular discipline that
began, "Ohio Wesleyan University seeks black applicants for a
tenure-track position." (The *Chronicle of Higher Education* refused
to include the provision that stipulated the job was only for
blacks.) "We were told we had two years to recruit a black person,"
a faculty member said. "If we didn't, we would lose the position.
It could not be used for someone who is white." At the University
of California, Los Angeles (UCLA), the Political Science Department ran an ad that specifically "invites nominations and applications from outstanding minority and female candidates."

May a college or university advertise in a way that automatically disqualifies members of the majority population? The U.S.
Equal Employment Opportunity Commission has stated: *Employers are prohibited from structuring their job advertisements in such a
way as to indicate that a group or groups of people would be excluded from*

consideration for employment on one of the bases set out in Title VII, which includes race. On the face of it, the ads (unless Ohio Wesleyan and UCLA had been under a court order to hire minorities to fill positions as a remedy to past identifiable discrimination) would appear to violate Title VII. However, such language as "Minorities and Women Are Encouraged to Apply" would be permitted by EEOC. This is more than a semantic quibble. It is the difference between an ad that does not bar applications from nonminority candidates and one that invites only minority candidates, implying that if nonminorities apply, they will not be considered. Last September, the head of the faculty search committee in Sociology at Wayne State University informed her colleagues that the two new authorized positions "*must* [her emphasis] be filled by a minority person" and that if the positions are not given to a member of an underrepresented minority group, the department "will not be able to make any hires." The memo did not make clear if university officials had directed her to adopt this policy. Apart from whether such a policy can be constitutionally sustained, one wonders if ads for these positions will be candid in indicating that "whites need not apply."

An issue seldom discussed publicly but of concern nonetheless is the extent to which the commitment to increase the number of blacks on faculties through racially preferential hiring will always coexist with the maintenance of high academic standards. Put another way, are colleges hiring some blacks with credentials weaker than those of the best white candidates? At Wayne State's Law School this past year, the administration informed the faculty that it would not authorize a position for a white candidate who had superior credentials until an offer was made to a black candidate already under consideration. "But his qualifications didn't even come close to those of our first choice," said a law faculty member. "So we made the black candidate an offer, who turned us down. Only then did we get approval to make an offer to the person we really wanted." He went on to say that the prospect of lowering standards in the search for more minorities is troubling. "That's the next step," he said. "There'll be less emphasis given to a candidate who served on the law review or who has worked in a law firm. These are things we normally look for. In short, there'll be changes in the academic criteria we have always considered to be good predictors of future academic success on a law school faculty." Meanwhile, in an August 1989 memo, the provost told the Law School that in authorizing a fall 1990 tenure-track appointment, "the position must be filled by a minority faculty person."

At most leading universities, the academic departments look for candidates who have already published or will soon publish influential articles and books. However, the pool of blacks who meet these scholarly criteria is very limited, which has led some affirmative-actionists to denounce traditional standards. But down that road lie thorny problems. For example, how far, and for how long, would a department's faculty have to live with what could become a double standard of evaluation? In colleges and universities where scholarly research and publication are a basic norm, are affirmative-action appointments to be exempted from these standards? If the percentage of articles submitted to and accepted by professional journals from black faculty continues to be small, should the long-standing practice of "blind" refereeing be replaced by a doctrine of "preferential compensation" that would lead editors to accept articles that would otherwise be rejected? The question is not entirely hypothetical. The Detroit Symphony recently found itself under attack because its self-instituted "blind" auditions—originally imposed to guarantee against race or gender discrimination—have not produced the requisite number of black musicians.

And what happens if a minority person who has been given a faculty appointment that can lead to tenure proves inadequate— but his (or her) ethnic group on campus demands that he be retained? A serious implication of undefined, irrelevant, or non-academic criteria is that they set the stage for the special claims of minority groups that only they are able to understand and pass judgment on members of their groups. There have already been demands on some campuses that black faculty be granted tenure as a form of affirmative action. At the University of Michigan, the United Coalition Against Racism has demanded that all black professors be given immediate tenure and special pay incentives. However, many black faculty members who presently have tenure strongly oppose this, knowing that it is not only condescending but that it diminishes their own legitimate and hard-won accomplishments. Gertrude Himmelfarb, the highly respected historian, has put it well: "If black faculty members are appointed, they should have the satisfaction of knowing (and having it known by their colleagues) that they were appointed on the basis of intellectual achievements and professional qualifications, not to fill a racial quota."

The use of double standards is not, of course, confined to blacks. Colleges and universities have been bending the admissions rules for athletes, children of alumni, and others for a long time. But as sociologist Christopher Jencks has observed, the long-run effects for blacks are especially pernicious. "As more and more blacks benefit at one point or another from reverse discrimination, fewer and fewer know how they would do if people stopped making special allowances for their presumed handicaps." White stereotypes about black incompetence also grow stronger, and "what once looked to liberal whites like a temporary transitional problem now looks like a permanent condition." The time has come, says Jencks, to insist that "no affirmative-action program should be adopted whose *de facto* result is reverse discrimination."

As charges of racism have mounted on campuses, many institutions have passed resolutions and announced plans to hire more black and other minority faculty who, it is true, are not heavily represented. The University of Wisconsin has agreed to find 70 new minority faculty members by 1991. Williams College set minority faculty hiring quotas of 20 percent by the early 1990s. Stanford University's president has called for 30 new minority faculty members over the next ten years. Duke University wants each of its 50 departments to hire at least one new black faculty member by 1993. And so on. But there is a problem. In the last ten years, there has been a substantial decline in the number of blacks earning doctoral degrees: of the 31,770 Ph.D.s earned in the United States in 1986, only 3.6 percent went to black Americans, 26.5 percent fewer than those awarded in 1977. Furthermore, less than half (272 of 547 black Ph.D.s) had plans for academic careers, compared to over two-thirds in 1975. The pool of black Ph.D.s has shrunk to its lowest level since 1975 and shows no immediate signs of recovery. So, colleges and universities will find it increasingly difficult to make promises they can keep about hiring more black faculty. Which poses some critical questions: What happens if they discover they can't meet their targets? Will they insist that their commitment to antidiscrimination and "equal rights for all" must now be converted to more aggressive affirmative-action policies that give precedence to race in faculty selection because numbers have now become even more urgent as ends in themselves? And how long will it then be before they move openly to a policy of hiring individuals whose scholarly credentials are less impressive than those of other applicants?

Affirmative action is not simply a policy that yields gains and benefits. It also entails demonstrable costs and consequences. To believe otherwise is to fail to understand that what one person gains under affirmative action may well be taken away from someone else. When there is such a collision of rights and conflict of principles, the important question is how one balances one's obligations. Thus the key to evaluating an affirmative-action program is how it is applied. For example, if a university fired a qualified white faculty member in order to hire a clearly unqualified black, it would be charged (and properly so) with violating every accepted standard of justice and fairness. But if a department, through a process in which all applicants are fairly reviewed and evaluated, hires a qualified black over an equally qualified white, no one could argue convincingly that the procedure was unjust. However, few could just as plausibly assert that either justice or the general good of the university would be served if a less-qualified candidate (black or white) were hired over someone who is fully and better qualified.

The issue is no longer whether there will be affirmative action but how much and for what purposes. What is especially mischievous is the notion that certain groups must invariably be given outright preference in faculty hiring solely on racial grounds, not only because race or sex or color are inappropriate tests of academic competence, but because such preference undermines the fundamental principle of individual merit and accomplishment that is central to the integrity of any self-respecting college or university. Our representatives construct policies that seek to provide social justice to a class, race, or ethnic group. But in recruiting a faculty, a college or university does not hire a class, race, or ethnic group. It hires a person.

There is broad agreement throughout higher education that a vigorous search must be made for highly qualified minorities. It is also strongly believed that the necessary resources must be made available to confirm that our society is committed to increasing opportunities for students of all races and backgrounds who want to get the Ph.D. and become college professors. The most promising hope lies in longer-term efforts that range from introducing minority students as early as possible to the opportunities available to them, to motivating those who show potential in college to pursue careers at the professional level so that the ranks of the truly qualified will be legitimately expanded. There should be guidance and assistance for people before they become incapacitated students. Good minds need to be rescued at the elementary and high-school levels lest they become dulled and ill-equipped to go on to college.

These goals deserve support because they are intended to eradicate attitudes that discourage disadvantaged and minority students from careers in the academic world. Perhaps the time has also come for college administrators and faculty to reaffirm publicly what most of them already know and admit privately— that what is not supportable is a straight racial line for making faculty appointments.

EDITOR'S INTRODUCTION

Quotas, or the threat of quotas, have been a potent tool in post-1960s racial politics. Affirmative action's detractors have often claimed that there is no distinction between affirmative action and quotas, while supporters have not always been able to portray that distinction to the satisfaction of those who feel that they would be adversely affected by preferences provided under some affirmative action programs.

One thing seems fairly certain from a reading of these articles: although at its inception affirmative action was designed to affect the lives of women and people of color, its success, or failure, ultimately lies largely in its acceptance by white America.

This section explores white attitudes towards affirmative action. In the first selection, "You Ain't the Right Color, Pal," Frederick R. Lynch and William R. Beer, two critics of affirmative action, see such policies as "incompatible with concepts of justice and reward deeply rooted in human behavior," and they regard the white male as a victim of society. The second article, "Republicans May Have Found the Perfect Democrat-Slayer," written by *Business Week* reporters Paula Dwyer and Tim Smart, shows how the Republican party used affirmative action and the quota issue to its advantage in the last election. In the third piece, Shelby Steele, writing in *The American Scholar,* calls affirmative action the result of an exaggerated white guilt that is based on self-interest and therefore detrimental to the condition of blacks in America. Finally, in "Another Look at Affirmative Action," Richard Drinan of Georgetown University's Law Center strongly endorses affirmative action and states that those opposed to it "have the burden of offering an alternative that will advance the position of blacks at least as much as affirmative action has done."

YOU AIN'T THE RIGHT COLOR, PAL[1]

One of the sleeper political forces in America is the growing sense of grievance among younger working-class and middle-

[1]Reprint of an article by Frederick R. Lynch, research associate, Claremont McKenna College and William R. Beer, professor of sociology, Brooklyn College. *Policy Review,* Number 51:64–67, 1990.

class white males most affected by affirmative action preferences. These policies were originally designed to ensure equal opportunities for blacks. Now, in the name of proportional representation for an expanding list of minority groups, they have created new forms of discrimination. A growing body of public opinion data, newspaper reports, anecdotal evidence, and sociological research suggests that whites feel frustrated and unfairly victimized by affirmative action preferences. The political and social consequences of such frustration are uncertain, but they may be contributing to racial polarization on many campuses, in workplaces, and in political life.

Public opinion polls consistently show that whites favor affirmative action in the form of compensatory training but overwhelmingly oppose preferential treatment and quotas for minorities in hiring and school admissions. According to a CBS/*New York Times* poll in 1977, 68 percent of whites favored government help for people who had suffered from a history of discrimination. This approval has continued into the Reagan-Bush years. A 1984 Harris poll found that 67.6 percent of whites accepted the idea of "affirmative action" when it excluded quotas.

On the other hand, whites reject anything less than equal opportunity for individuals. In March 1988, a *Newsweek*/Gallup poll asked: "Because of past discrimination, should qualified blacks receive preference over equally qualified whites in such matters as getting into college or getting jobs or not?" In results consistent with 20 years of polling data, 80 percent of whites (and 50 percent of blacks) responded, "should not."

In a 1984 telephone survey of registered voters by Gordon Black Associates, 1 out of 10 white males said that they had personally experienced reverse discrimination. The 1986 National Election Study by the University of Michigan's Institute for Social Research discovered that well over half of whites believed whites have been hurt by affirmative action in hiring and school admissions. When whites were asked if a white person would be refused admission to a school while an equally or less qualified black was accepted, 27.6 percent responded "very likely" and 41.4 percent said "somewhat likely," for a positive total response of 69 percent. A similar question was asked about hiring; 26.6 percent of whites responded "very likely" and 48.3 percent said "somewhat likely"—a total of 75 percent—that a white would lose out.

The National Election Study also asked whites what they estimated the chances were that they or someone in their family would suffer reverse discrimination. In school admissions, 12.5 percent thought this very likely and 30 percent thought it somewhat likely, while in hiring and promotions, the percentages were 12.4 and 28.7 percent, respectively—for a total of more than 40 percent in both categories.

White responses to affirmative action quotas are patterned in part by social class, union membership, and education level. Working-class whites have been more overt and organized in articulating responses. Many of the definitive cases decided by the courts have involved challenges brought by unionized police, fire fighters, and correctional officers. Response among middle-class whites, especially those with some college education, has been more muted and fragmented.

A related factor affecting response of whites has been their institutional location. Affirmative action preferences have most affected younger whites in public sector organizations and corporations with government contracts. Preferences have also been implemented with increasing candor and aggressiveness in universities and colleges.

Campus Standards: Separate and Unequal

Andrew Hacker has joined many other analysts in observing that affirmative action has a bold new look on university campuses. As he wrote in the *New York Review of Books* last October, universities are admitting blacks and Latinos with substantially lower academic qualifications than many of the whites and Asians they are turning away. A dean of admissions told Hacker: "We take in more in the groups with weaker credentials and make it harder for those with stronger credentials."

Hacker and others have spotlighted major ethnic changes in the undergraduate enrollment at the University of California's Berkeley campus. Under pressure from the state legislature, Berkeley administrators quadrupled the percentage of blacks and Latinos in the freshman class in less than a decade—from 8 to 31 percent. There has been a corresponding, dramatic decrease in the percentage of whites—from over 60 percent to 32 percent.

According to Hacker, University of California administrators realized that "the only way to raise [black and Latino] representation would be to waive the admission rules, and this was done." Most whites and Asians were admitted on the basis of grades and test scores—about 50 percent of each freshman class. The other

50 percent (including most blacks and Latinos) were admitted in a second category stressing "other criteria"—mainly race and ethnicity. About 6 percent of each incoming class consists of "special action," less-than-qualified students. A similar transformation has occurred at UCLA.

Some Asian groups have openly and vigorously protested these arrangements. White protest has been more fragmented and subtle. Some parents of whites reportedly threatened *Bakke*-style lawsuits. But other whites may be "voting with their feet"—as whites did in busing battles—and going elsewhere. Applications from potential white students at Berkeley were down 15 percent from last year.

A cover story in the April 26, 1989, *Chronicle of Higher Education* observed that, on many campuses, white "students believe that minority group members today enjoy unfair advantages and that whites are being victimized by efforts intended to correct past discrimination." Said Michael L. Davis, director of the University of Texas Minority Information Center: "There is an undercurrent of antagonism, maybe even frustration, with programs and monies specifically set aside for minorities." Paul Bartley, the chairman of the Young Conservatives of Texas, argues that it is "inherently racist" to single out blacks or Hispanics for special treatment. At Pennsylvania State University, blacks not only get special preference in admissions, but they are also eligible for $500 "Black Achievement Awards" for maintaining a "C" average and $1,000 for maintaining a "C+" average. "When I hear stuff like that, it really angers me," said a white female student at the school.

Affirmative action quotas have become a central issue of a newly formed white students association at Temple University. University of Michigan students and alumni have registered vigorous objections to lowering admission standards for minorities as well as proposals to recruit out-of-state minority undergraduates to fill quotas. Among white graduate students at many institutions, there is growing irritation at clear favoritism in financial aid for minority students. For instance, the California State University system offers minorities and a few white females loans of up to $30,000 to pursue doctorates at other institutions, which are forgiven if they return to teach in the CSU system for five years. White males are ineligible; Asian males are also excluded in most instances.

Quiet Alienation

Frederick R. Lynch conducted 32 in-depth interviews with mostly middle-class white males who considered themselves reverse discrimination victims. Most avoided open complaint or protest out of fear of not being believed or that they would be labeled racist. The majority simply acquiesced in their treatment with varying degrees of resignation and anger.

Most of Lynch's subjects voiced temporary, if not long-term, frustration and cynicism about social institutions. "A lot of us were sold a bill of goods," complained a California state middle-management worker. "We were told if you went to college you could write your own ticket. But . . . affirmative action has lowered standards to the point where education almost counts against you." Many felt alienated from a society that refused to acknowledge their victimization. A white teacher, transferred to a distant school in a racial balancing plan, bitterly commented: "My friends couldn't handle this. They experienced cognitive dissonance. They didn't want to be seen as racists." Although victims of reverse discrimination were cynical or angry toward social and political institutions, almost no one in Lynch's study expressed hostility towards minorities *per se*.

Six of Lynch's subjects quit or resigned from the organizations that discriminated against them. Three circumvented affirmative action barriers within their organizations by various means. Only three filed lawsuits. (None were successful.) No government agency offered redress.

Firehouse Suits

In contrast to the disorganized response of middle-class whites, working-class white police and fire fighters in Cleveland, Detroit, Los Angeles, San Francisco, Birmingham, and a host of other cities have taken legal action against quotas imposed by courts or administrators. Several key Supreme Court decisions on affirmative action have involved police and fire fighters (notably *Memphis Fire fighters* v. *Stotts* [1984], *Local 93 of the International Association of Firefighters* v. *City of Cleveland* [1986], *Local 28 of the Sheet Metal Workers* v. *Equal Employment Opportunity Commission* [1986], and *Martin* v. *Wilks*, [1989]). Correctional officers have also launched such lawsuits. Many disputes involved attempts by ad-

ministrators to negate or adjust minority test-score results on entry-level or promotional exams. For example, 200 minority candidates who failed a 1983 sergeants exam in the New York City
Police Department were nonetheless promoted to boost the proportion of minority officers. New York state correctional officers
sued when administrators adjusted test scores of minority officers
to increase the pass rate on a promotional exam. (Such practices
were accidentally uncovered in the Boston Police Department
when it was recently discovered that two white police officers had
falsified their racial identities and obtained entry to the force with
scores approximately 20 percentile points below the level required for whites.)

Unions have also been active in contesting reverse discrimination in layoff situations. Teachers' unions in Boston and Michigan
have entered reverse discrimination cases when whites with greater seniority were laid off, while blacks with less seniority were
retained.

Availability of union legal staffs may have been one reason for
more active and effective blue-collar response. But another is that
police, fire fighters, correctional officers, and teachers have borne
much of the sacrifice of affirmative action. New hires and those
seeking their first promotions have been most severely affected.

Shocker for Democrats

Blue-collar whites' outrage over use of preferences for blacks
and immigrants was discovered by Stanley Greenberg in research
sponsored by the Democratic Party in 1985. The purpose of the
research was to discover the roots of Democratic defection to
Ronald Reagan in the 1980 and 1984 presidential elections. The
moderator of a discussion group of blue-collar whites asked them
"Who do you think gets the raw deal?" The answers:

"We do."

"The middle-class white guy."

"The working middle class."

" 'Cause women get advantages, the Hispanics get advantages,
Orientals get advantages. Everybody but the white male race gets
advantages now."

From another section of Greenberg's report:

"I have been here all my life working, paying taxes and the
whole shot, and I can't start my own business unless I have 30
percent down on whatever I want to buy. I have experience on the

job, I have put in for openings, and they have come right out and told me in personnel that the government has come down and said that, 'I can't have the job because they have to give it to the minorities.'"

"I know what you are talking about. I tried to apply for a business loan and yesterday they said, 'No go. Forget it, you just ain't the right color, pal.'"

Greenberg and his Democratic sponsors reported being stunned by these results. Much to their chagrin, fury over affirmative action was one of the top concerns of white, working-class voters. Similar data were obtained from a "Democrats Listening to America" poll of 5,500 voters in 1985.

After the 1988 elections, influential Democrats began to speak more openly of the threat posed by affirmative action quotas to the traditional Democratic Party alliance of white working classes and minorities. In the *New York Times Magazine* Joseph Califano, President Carter's Secretary of Health and Human Services, warned that whites view affirmative action as "unfair pandering to black constituents. They view such a permanent commitment as founded not on need or social justice but on a guilt they refuse to accept. . . . Continued support of programs that are not achieving their goals may aggravate rather than ease racial tension."

Angry at the System

Racial incidents in male-oriented organizations—such as college fraternities and police departments—are perhaps the result of racial prejudices, combined with the verbal jousting and hazing common in such "macho" environments. But they also may be the expression of frustration with affirmative action. Such incidents have occurred in northern, liberal universities with vigorous commitment to affirmative action preferences—such as the Universities of Michigan, Wisconsin, and Massachusetts. Police and fire departments in some "progressive" cities—such as San Francisco and New York—have also experienced such incidents in the context of affirmative action disputes.

We do not dismiss the possibility that in some of these incidents old-fashioned racial prejudice may be masquerading as opposition to affirmative action. The recent murder of a black man in Brooklyn's Bensonhurst section is a reminder of the persistence of conventional racism. Nonetheless, we would suggest that white anger over affirmative action preferences can be examined independently of old-fashioned racism with elementary tools of behavioral science.

Treating people differently because of their race, origin, or gender violates what Harvard's George Homans termed the law of distributive justice. According to this principle, people feel that their rewards should be proportional to their "investments"—educational level, grades, test scores, seniority, experience, and other measurable qualities. If others with less training, ability, or education are granted equal or superior rewards, frustration and anger are the likely outcomes.

That arbitrarily assigned group preferences might result in anger and hostility toward favored groups was confirmed in a social psychology experiment conducted by Stephen Johnson of Ball State University. In a small group laboratory setting, Johnson asked 32 white male college students to solve a puzzle. The game was rigged: all subjects would lose. Half of them were told they had lost to a fictitious competitor because the latter's solution of the puzzle was deemed better by the experimenter. The other half were told after they had solved the puzzle that the competitor had been assigned a bonus score based on economic deprivation. In addition, half of the subjects were told they had lost to a black competitor, half to a white competitor. Subjects expressed little hostility when they lost to blacks or whites whose performance was superior. They expressed considerable hostility, however, toward victors who had been assigned a bonus because of their backgrounds, with the greatest hostility toward blacks—a classic "reverse discrimination" situation.

On the other hand, all middle-class white males interviewed by Lynch, and most working-class white males studied by Greenberg, directed their anger toward a system of unfair rewards—not minorities *per se*. Johnson did not measure hostility toward the experimenter or the system of rewards, so we do not know what those results would have been.

Legitimate Grievances

Most civil-rights leaders championed affirmative action on the grounds that it was necessary to overcome persistent discrimination against blacks in the workplace. The goal was nondiscrimination.

However, analysts have increasingly recognized that affirmative action programs have changed. Race-consciousness, not race neutrality, is encouraged. Many corporations, government agencies, and universities are allocating positions on the basis of race and ethnicity in order to achieve proportional representation for a variety of minority and immigrant groups. The *New Republic*'s Hendrik Hertzberg last summer bared an underlying assumption of group-preference policy when he argued that an entire generation of white males must be sacrificed for the hope of future racial peace and social stability.

Obviously, many white males feel the affirmative action sacrifices have already been made. Indeed, as preferences are brought to bear on undergraduates, we are entering a second generation of affirmative action.

Americans must recognize and examine the consequences of these policies. Recent Supreme Court decisions have indicated that quotas or set-asides may not survive constitutional scrutiny. We have argued that the policies are incompatible with concepts of justice and reward deeply rooted in human behavior.

It has been a mistake to ignore the legitimate grievances of whites who believe that affirmative action programs are penalizing them for injustices they personally did not commit. Continued refusal to discuss problems wrought by affirmative action in recognized national forums invites political polarization, exploitation by political opportunists, the growth of fringe politics, and, perhaps, a political backlash.

The persistent white racism in many American communities deserves condemnation. But it is inappropriate to attribute to old-fashioned prejudice all of whites' unhappiness with affirmative action. The claims of unfair treatment, the expressions of injury and personal wrong, the feelings of alienation and victimization are in many cases genuine. They deserve sympathy from all Americans inspired by Martin Luther King's dream of a society where a man is judged by the content of his character, not the color of his skin.

REPUBLICANS MAY HAVE FOUND THE PERFECT DEMOCRAT-SLAYER[2]

The Democrats are about to discover the dark side of the fairness issue. During the recent campaign, they put Republicans

[2]Article by Paula Dwyer, with Tim Smart. Reprinted from December 3, 1990 issue of *Business Week* by special permission, copyright © 1990 by McGraw-Hill, Inc.

on the defensive by portraying the GOP as the party of millionaires. But Republicans in a half-dozen states scored big by tying their opponents to "unfair" racial quotas.

That's what you call successful test-marketing. In 1992, the quota issue will get a full-scale national rollout, promises William J. Bennett, President Bush's choice to head the Republican National Committee. And the Democrats are ill-prepared to defend themselves.

In tight races from North Carolina to California, Republican candidates helped their cause by equating Democrat-backed affirmative-action programs with hiring quotas. "This is an issue that not only polarizes the races but plays on the economic insecurities people are feeling right now," says Democratic pollster Geoffrey Garin.

The GOP's opening came on Oct. 22, when President Bush made good on his promise to veto a civil rights bill. The President said that the measure, designed to reverse Supreme Court decisions that made it harder for minorities and women to win job-discrimination suits, was "a quota bill." While the legislation did not mandate quotas, business groups argued that if it became law, companies would resort to numerical hiring targets to protect themselves from lawsuits.

The veto was a bitter disappointment to civil rights leaders, whom Bush had courted for two years. But the President was willing to sacrifice his relations with black leaders to help Republican candidates in a handful of tough races.

Senator Jesse A. Helms, locked in a fierce struggle with black Democrat Harvey B. Gantt, was a major beneficiary. As soon as the President signed the veto message, the North Carolina Republican unleashed a hard-hitting television spot that showed a white hand crumpling a job-rejection letter. "You needed that job," said the voice-over. "And you were the best qualified. But they had to give it to a minority because of a racial quota. Is that really fair?" The ad helped Helms win 63% of the white vote— and the election.

Crude racial appeals paid off in Alabama and Louisiana, too. It would be easy for Democrats to dismiss these cases as the revenge of unreconstructed segregationists. But far more worrisome for Democrats is the success Republican Pete Wilson had in the California governor's race by attacking Dianne Feinstein's plan to give more state jobs to women, blacks, and Hispanics. The attacks pulled white males and Asian-Americans over to Wilson's column.

The success of Helms and the others hasn't deterred the Democrats from preparing to reprise this year's civil rights struggle. After all, blacks are a core constituency for the Democrats. Party leaders have promised that reintroducing the vetoed legislation is a top priority in the new Congress. The Administration is likely to counter with a stripped-down version that eliminates the sections that business objects to most. But with increased majorities in both houses, liberal Democrats hope to pass the original measure over Bush's veto.

Win or lose—and the odds are still that they'll lose—Democrats seem determined to give the GOP another shot at the quota issue. Bennett is raring for a fight. Those who criticize Helms's "rejection-slip" ad, Bennett told reporters on Nov. 19, "have got to realize that most Americans are troubled by this issue." He's prepared to make affirmative action a part of the 1992 Presidential campaign, if the Democrats push civil rights.

Democratic liberals scoff at this possibility, but fear of quotas is precisely the sort of "wedge" issue that the GOP can exploit to splinter the Democratic coalition. And in an economic slump, the question of preferential hiring gains potency. "President Bush is recognizing that the quota issue is important to holding on to white votes that, in times of recession, would vote Democratic," says Clint Bolick, director of the conservative Landmark Center for Civil Rights.

Pollster Celinda C. Lake believes her fellow Democrats will remain suspect to working-class whites as long as the party's message seems targeted to the underclass. Lake has found that in focus groups, many blue-collar workers are quick to complain about reverse discrimination. "Democrats have failed to articulate a broader economic view," Lake says. "That's scary when the economy's going down the tubes."

Given Lake's findings, it should be no surprise to Democrats in '92 if George Bush takes off the gloves and starts bashing the opposition for supporting quotas. He showed a similar bare-knuckles flair in 1988, when he turned furloughed black prisoner Willie Horton into a symbol of Democratic permissiveness. Bush won't have Horton to kick around next election. But with the quota issue, he might not need him.

WHITE GUILT[3]

I don't remember hearing the phrase "white guilt" very much before the mid-1960s. Growing up black in the 1950s, I never had the impression that whites were much disturbed by guilt when it came to blacks. When I would stray into the wrong restaurant in pursuit of a hamburger, it didn't occur to me that the waitress was unduly troubled by guilt when she asked me to leave. I can see now that possibly she was, but then all I saw was her irritability at having to carry out so unpleasant a task. If there was guilt, it was mine for having made an imposition of myself. I can remember feeling a certain sympathy for such people, as if I was victimizing them by drawing them out of an innocent anonymity into the unasked for role of racial policemen. Occasionally they came right out and asked me to feel sorry for them. A caddymaster at a country club told my brother and me that he was doing us a favor by not letting us caddy at this white club and that we should try to understand his position, "put yourselves in my shoes." Our color had brought this man anguish and, if a part of that anguish was guilt, it was not as immediate to me as my own guilt. I smiled at the man to let him know he shouldn't feel bad and then began my long walk home. Certainly I also judge him a coward, but in that era his cowardice was something I had to absorb.

In the 1960s, particularly the black-is-beautiful late 1960s, this absorption of another's cowardice was no longer necessary. The lines of moral power, like plates in the earth, had shifted. White guilt became so palpable you could see it on people. At the time what it looked like to my eyes was a remarkable loss of authority. And what whites lost in authority, blacks gained. You cannot feel guilty about anyone without giving away power to them. Suddenly, this huge vulnerability had opened up in whites and, as a black, you had the power to step right into it. In fact, black power all but demanded that you do so. What shocked me in the late 1960s, after the helplessness I had felt in the fifties, was that guilt had changed the nature of the white man's burden from the administration of inferiors to the uplift of equals—from the obligations of dominance to the urgencies of repentance.

[3]Reprint of an article by Shelby Steele, professor at San Jose State University. Copyright © 1990 American Scholar. Reprinted with permission.

I think what made the difference between the fifties and six-
ties, at least as far as white guilt was concerned, was that whites
underwent an archetypal Fall. Because of the immense turmoil of
the civil rights movement, and later the black-power movement,
whites were confronted for more than a decade with their willingness to participate in, or comply with, the oppression of blacks,
their indifference to human suffering and denigration, their ca-
pacity to abide evil for their own benefit and in the defiance of
their own sacred principles. The 1964 Civil Rights Bill that be-
stowed equality under the law on blacks was also, in a certain
sense, an admission of white guilt. Had white society not been
wrong, there would have been no need for such a bill. In this bill
the nation acknowledged its fallenness, its lack of racial innocence, and confronted the incriminating self-knowledge that it
had rationalized for many years a flagrant injustice. Denial is a
common way of handling guilt, but in the 1960s there was little
will left for denial except in the most recalcitrant whites. With this
defense lost there was really only one road back to innocence—
through actions and policies that would bring redemption.

In the 1960s the need for white redemption from racial guilt
became the most powerful, yet unspoken, element in America's
social-policy-making process, first giving rise to the Great Society
and then to a series of programs, policies, and laws that sought to
make black equality and restitution a national mission. Once
America could no longer deny its guilt, it went after redemption,
or at least the look of redemption, and did so with a vengeance.
Yet today, some twenty years later, study after study tells us that
by many measures the gap between blacks and whites is widening
rather than narrowing. A University of Chicago study indicates
that segregation is more entrenched in American cities today than
ever imagined. A National Research Council study notes the "status of blacks relative to whites (in housing and education) has
stagnated or regressed since the early seventies." A follow-up to
the famous Kerner Commission Report warns that blacks are as
much at risk today of becoming a "nation within a nation" as we
were twenty years ago, when the original report was made.

I think the white need for redemption has contributed to this
tragic situation by shaping our policies regarding blacks in ways
that may deliver the look of innocence to society and its institutions but that do very little actually to uplift blacks. The specific
effect of this hidden need has been to bend social policy more
toward reparation for black oppression than toward the much
harder and more mundane work of black uplift and develop-

ment. Rather than facilitate the development of blacks to achieve parity with whites, these programs and policies—affirmative action is a good example—have tended to give blacks special entitlements that in many cases are of no use because blacks lack the development that would put us in a position to take advantage of them. I think the reason there has been more entitlement than development is (along with black power) the unacknowledged white need for redemption—not true redemption, which would have concentrated policy on black development, but the appearance of redemption, which requires only that society, in the name of development, seem to be paying back its former victims with preferences. One of the effects of entitlements, I believe, has been to encourage in blacks a dependency both on entitlements and on the white guilt that generates them. Even when it serves ideal justice, bounty from another man's guilt weakens. While this is not the only factor in black "stagnation" and "regression," I believe it is one very potent factor.

It is easy enough to say that white guilt too often has the effect of bending social policies in the wrong direction. But what exactly is this guilt, and how does it work in American life?

I think white guilt, in its broad sense, springs from a knowledge of ill-gotten advantage. More precisely, it comes from the juxtaposition of this knowledge with the inevitable gratitude one feels for being white rather than black in America. Given the moral instincts of human beings, it is all but impossible to enjoy an ill-gotten advantage, much less to feel at least secretly grateful for it, without consciously or unconsciously experiencing guilt. If, as Kierkegaard writes, "innocence is ignorance," then guilt must always involve knowledge. White Americans *know* that their historical advantage comes from the subjugation of an entire people. So, even for whites today for whom racism is anathema, there is no escape from the knowledge that makes for guilt. Racial guilt simply accompanies the condition of being white in America.

I do not believe that this guilt is a crushing anguish for most whites, but I do believe it constitutes a continuing racial vulnerability—an openness to racial culpability—that is a thread in white life, sometimes felt, sometimes not, but ever present as a potential feeling. In the late 1960s almost any black could charge this vulnerability with enough current for a white person to feel it. I had a friend who had developed this activity into a sort of specialty. I don't think he meant to be mean, though certainly he was mean. I think he was, in that hyperbolic era, exhilarated by the discovery that his race, which had long been a liability, now gave him a certain edge—that white guilt was the true force behind black power. To feel this power he would sometimes set up what he called "race experiments." Once I watched him stop a white businessman in the men's room of a large hotel and convince him to increase his tip to the black attendant from one to twenty dollars.

My friend's tactic was very simple, even corny. Out of the attendant's earshot he asked the man simply to look at the attendant, a frail, elderly, and very dark man in a starched white smock that made the skin on his neck and face look as leathery as a turtle's. He sat listlessly, pathetically, on a straight-backed chair next to a small table on which sat a stack of hand towels and a silver plate for tips. Since the attendant offered no service whatever beyond the handing out of towels, one could only conclude the hotel management offered his lowly presence as flattery to their patrons, as an opportunity for that easy noblesse oblige that could reassure even the harried and weary traveling salesman of his superior station. My friend was quick to make this point to the businessman and to say that no white man would do in this job. But when the businessman put the single back in his wallet and took out a five, my friend only sneered. Did he understand the tragedy of a life spent this way, of what it must be like to earn one's paltry living as a symbol of inferiority? And did he realize that his privilege as an affluent white businessman (ironically he had just spent the day trying to sell a printing press to the Black Muslims for their newspaper *Mohammed Speaks*) was connected to the deprivation of this man and others like him?

But then my friend made a mistake that ended the game. In the heat of argument, which until then had only been playfully challenging, he inadvertently mentioned his father. This stopped the victim cold and his eyes turned inward. "What about your father?" the businessman asked. My friend replied, "He had a hard life, that's all." "How did he have a hard life?" the businessman asked. Now my friend was on the defensive. I knew he did not get along with his father, a bitter man who worked nights in a factory and demanded that the house be dark and silent all day. My friend blamed his father's bitterness on racism, but I knew he had not meant to exploit his own pain in this silly "experiment." Things had gotten too close to home, but he didn't know how to get out of the situation without losing face. Now, caught in his own trap, he did what he least wanted to do. He gave forth the rage he truly felt to a white stranger in a public men's room. "My father never had a chance," he said with the kind of anger that could easily turn to tears. "He never had a freakin' chance. Your father had all the goddamn chances, and you know he did. You sell printing presses to black people and make thousands and your father probably lives down in Fat City, Florida, all because you're white." On and on he went in this vein, using—against all that was honorable in him—his own profound racial pain to extract a flash of guilt from a white man he didn't even know.

He got more than a flash. The businessman was touched. His eyes became mournful, and finally he simply said, "You're right. Your people got a raw deal." He took a twenty dollar bill from his wallet and walked over and dropped it in the old man's tip plate. When he was gone my friend and I could not look at the old man, nor could we look at each other.

It is obvious that this was a rather shameful encounter for all concerned—my friend and I, as his silent accomplice, trading on our racial pain, tampering with a stranger for no reason, and the stranger then buying his way out of the situation for twenty dollars, a sum that was generous by one count and cheap by another. It was not an encounter of people but of historical grudges and guilts. Yet, when I think about it now twenty years later, I see that it had all the elements of a paradigm that I believe has been very much at the heart of racial policy-making in America since the 1960s.

My friend did two things that made this businessman vulnerable to his guilt—that brought his guilt into the situation as a force. First he put this man in touch with his own knowledge of his ill-gotten advantage as a white. The effect of this was to disallow the man any pretense of racial innocence, to let him know that, even if he was not the sort of white who used the word *nigger* around the dinner table, he still had reason to feel racial guilt. But, as disarming as this might have been, it was too abstract to do much more than crack open this man's vulnerability, to expose him to the logic of white guilt. This was the five-dollar, intellectual sort of guilt. The twenty dollars required something more visceral. In achieving this, the second thing my friend did was something he had not intended to do, something that ultimately brought him as much shame as he was doling out: He made a display of his own racial pain and anger. (What brought him shame was not the pain and anger, but his trading on them for what turned out to be a mere twenty bucks.) The effect of this display was to reinforce the man's knowledge of ill-gotten advantage, to give credibility and solidity to it by putting a face on it. Here was human testimony, a young black beside himself at the thought of his father's racially constricted life. The pain of one man evidenced the knowledge of the other. When the businessman listened to my friend's pain, his racial guilt—normally only one source of guilt lying dormant among others—was called out like a neglected debt he would finally have to settle. An ill-gotten advantage is not hard to bear— it can be marked up to fate—until it touches the genuine human pain it has brought into the world. This is the pain that hardens guilty knowledge.

Such knowledge is a powerful influence when it becomes conscious. What makes it so powerful is the element of fear that guilt always carries, the fear of what the guilty knowledge says about us. Guilt makes us afraid for ourselves, and thus generates as much self-preoccupation as concern for others. The nature of this preoccupation is always the redemption of innocence, the reestablishment of good feeling about oneself.

In this sense, the fear for the self that is buried in all guilt is a pressure toward selfishness. It can lead us to put our own need for innocence above our concern for the problem that made us feel guilt in the first place. But this fear for the self does not only inspire selfishness; it also becomes a pressure to *escape* the guilt-inducing situation. When selfishness and escapism are at work, we are no longer interested in the source of our guilt and, therefore, no longer concerned with an authentic redemption from it. Then we only want the look of redemption, the gesture of concern that will give us the appearance of innocence and escape from the situation. Obviously the businessman did not put twenty dollars in the tip plate because he thought it would uplift black Americans. He did it selfishly for the appearance of concern and for the escape it afforded him.

This is not to say that guilt is never the right motive for doing good works or showing concern, only that it is a very dangerous one because of its tendency to draw us into self-preoccupation and escapism. Guilt is a civilizing emotion when the fear for the self that it carries is contained—a containment that allows guilt to be more selfless and that makes genuine concern possible. I think this was the kind of guilt that, along with the other forces, made the 1964 Civil Rights Bill possible. But since then I believe too many of our social policies related to race have been shaped by the fearful underside of guilt.

Black power evoked white guilt and made it a force in Ameri-

can institutions, very much in the same way as my friend brought
it to life in the businessman. Few people volunteer for guilt. Usually others make us feel it. It was the expression of black anger
and pain that hardened the guilty knowledge of white ill-gotten
advantage. And black power—whether from militant fringe
groups, the civil rights establishment, or big city political cam-
paigns—knew exactly the kind of white guilt it was after. It wanted to trigger the kind of white guilt in which whites fear for their
own decency and innocence; it wanted the guilt of white self-
preoccupation and escapism. Always at the heart of black power,
in whatever form, has been a profound anger at what was done to
blacks and an equally profound feeling that there should be rep-
arations. But a sober white guilt (in which fear for the self is still
contained) seeks a strict fairness—the 1964 Civil Rights Bill that
guaranteed equality under the law. It is of little value when one is
after more than fairness. So black power made its mission to have
whites fear for their innocence, to feel a visceral guilt from which
they would have to seek a more profound redemption. In such
redemption was the possibility of black reparation. Black power
upped the ante on white guilt.

With black power, all of the elements of the hidden paradigm
that shape America's race-related social policy were in place.
Knowledge of ill-gotten advantage could now be shown and deep-
ened by black power into the sort of guilt from which institutions
could only redeem themselves by offering more than fairness—
by offering forms of reparation and compensation for past injustice. I believe this bent our policies toward racial entitlements
at the expense of racial development. In 1964, one of the as-
surances Senator Hubert Humphrey and others had to give Congress to get the landmark Civil Rights Bill passed was that the bill
would not in any way require employers to use racial preferences
to rectify racial imbalances. But this was before the explosion of
black power in the late 1960s, before the hidden paradigm was set
in motion. After black power, racial preferences became the
order of the day.

If this paradigm brought blacks entitlements, it also brought
the continuation of the most profound problem in American society, the invisibility of blacks as a people. The white guilt that this
paradigm elicits is the kind of guilt that preoccupies whites with
their own innocence and pressures them toward escapism—twenty dollars in the plate and out the door. With this guilt, as opposed
to the contained guilt of genuine concern, whites tend to see only

their own need for quick redemption. Blacks then become a means to this redemption and, as such, they must be seen as generally "less than" others. Their needs are "special," "unique," "different." They are seen exclusively along the dimension of their victimization, so that they become "different" people with whom whites can negotiate entitlements but never fully see as people like themselves. Guilt that preoccupies people with their own innocence blinds them to those who make them feel guilty. This, of course, is not racism, and yet is has the same effect as racism since it makes blacks something of a separate species for whom normal standards and values do not automatically apply. . . .

I think effective racial policies can only come from the sort of white guilt where fear for the self is contained, so that genuine concern can ultimately emerge. The test for this healthy guilt is simply a heartfelt feeling of concern without any compromise of one's highest values and principles. But how can whites reach this more selfless form of guilt? I believe the only way is to slacken one's grip on innocence. Guilt has always been the lazy man's way to innocence—I feel guilt *because* I am innocent, and guilt confirms my innocence. It is the compulsion to think always of ourselves as innocent that binds us to self-preoccupied guilt. Whites in general, and particularly those public and private institutions (not necessarily white) that make racial policy, must not be so preoccupied with their image of innocence or, put another way, their public relations of good intentions. What is needed now is a new spirit of pragmatism in racial matters where blacks are viewed simply as American citizens who deserve complete fairness, and in some cases developmental assistance, but in no case special entitlements based on color. We need social policies that attack poverty rather than *black* poverty and that instill those values that make for self-reliance. The white message to blacks must be: America hurt you badly and that is wrong, but entitlements only prolong the hurt, while development overcomes it.

Selfish white guilt is really self-importance. It has no humility, and it asks for an unreasonable, egotistical innocence. Nothing diminishes a black more than this sort of guilt in a white, which to my mind amounts to a sort of moral colonialism. We used to say in the 1960s that at least in the South you knew where you stood. I always thought this was a little foolish, since I didn't like where I stood there. But I think one of the things we meant by this—at the time—was that the South had little investment in its racial innocence and that this was very liberating in an ironical sort of way. It meant there would be no entangling complications with white need. It gave us back ourselves. The selfishly guilty white person is drawn to what blacks least like in themselves—their suffering, victimization, and dependency. This is no good for anyone—black or white.

ANOTHER LOOK AT AFFIRMATIVE ACTION[4]

The controversy about affirmative action is becoming more complex and confusing. It is uncertain whether the negative attitude toward affirmative action on the part of the Reagan Administration or the Supreme Court decision concerning firefighters in Memphis last June will actually deter specific, ongoing programs employing affirmative action. But the climate of general acceptance of affirmative action may be shifting. It is therefore appropriate to discuss: 1) the meaning of the 6-3 Supreme Court decision in the Memphis firefighters case, 2) the extensive use of affirmative action in other nations and its incorporation into international law and 3) the progress made by the use of affirmative action since 1965.

In 1974, the city of Memphis signed a consent degree that settled a suit brought against the city by the Civil Rights Division of the U.S. Department of Justice. The city agreed to set aside 50 percent of all job vacancies for qualified black applicants. In 1980, the city also agreed to ensure that 20 percent of the promotions in each job classification be given to blacks.

In neither decree was there any reference to what would happen if some firefighters or others were laid off. In 1981, the city announced that projected budget deficits required a reduction in personnel and that the citywide seniority system would be followed. Of the 40 firefighting employees to be laid off, 25 were white and 15 were black.

The Federal District Court enjoined the city from following the seniority rule since it would be in essence inconsistent with the

[4]Reprint of an article by Robert F. Drinan, professor of law, Georgetown University Law Center. *America* 152:104–106, February 9, 1985. Reprinted with permission.

consent degree agreed to by the city. The Circuit Court of Appeals sustained the injunction, but on June 12, 1984, the United States Supreme Court reversed, holding that Federal courts had no power to impose on a city a policy that preferred affirmative action to seniority.

The Supreme Court decision can be viewed narrowly as not a curtailment of affirmative action but only as an insistence that Federal courts cannot go beyond their proper mandate. Lawyers for black employees will henceforth insist that agreements involving affirmative action provide specifically for the practices and priorities to be followed if it becomes necessary to cut back the work force.

A few statements in the Memphis decision can be construed as unfavorable to affirmative action. The fact is, however, that all of the Federal courts of appeals throughout the country are unanimous in holding the view that race-conscious affirmative relief is permissible under Title VII of the Civil Rights Act of 1965; that law permits the court to "order such affirmative action as may be appropriate, which may include, but is not limited to, reinstatement or hiring of employees . . . or any other equitable relief as the court deems appropriate." .

It is also clear that the Memphis decision did not reverse Bakke, the 1978 decision in which a majority of the Supreme Court wrote that "executive, judicial and Congressional action subsequent to the passage of Title VII did not bar the remedial use of race."

That "remedial use" of race has been recommended on the international level for many years and has become a part of international law. In 1963, the General Assembly of the United Nations began the drafting of the Declaration on the Elimination of All Forms of Racial Discrimination. With active support from the United States, this document was completed in 1965. In 1969, after the requisite number of nations ratified the declaration, it entered into force as a part of international law. In 1984, 107 nations had ratified the declaration—more ratifications than for any of the treaties that have emerged from the United Nations. Even though the U.S. Senate has never ratified the declaration, it is arguably binding on the United States.

Article 1, 4 of this declaration approves of affirmative action in these carefully crafted words: "Special measures taken for the sole purpose of securing adequate advancement of certain racial or ethnic groups or individuals requiring such protection as may

be necessary in order to ensure such groups or individuals equal
enjoyment or exercise of human rights and fundamental free-
doms shall not be deemed racial discrimination, provided, however, that such measures do not, as a consequence, lead to the
maintenance of separate rights for different racial groups and
that they shall not be continued after the objectives for which they
were taken have been achieved."

This statement clearly enunciates the principle that measures
designed to bring racial or ethnic groups into the mainstream
shall *not* be deemed to be discrimination or reverse discrimination. The one qualification is the clear understanding that the
privileges or preferences that have been extended will be removed as soon as they are no longer required.

It is unfortunate that this part of international law, which is
the product of some of the finest legal minds around the world,
has hardly ever entered into the heated discussion about affirmative action now going on in the United States.

This clear but careful endorsement of affirmative action
agreed to by over two-thirds of the nations of the earth is a significant factor in the very valuable volume on affirmative action published in May by the Rockefeller Foundation. This collection of 10
papers on affirmative action, by experts from nations that include
Malaysia, Nigeria, Israel and West Germany, demonstrates that in
numerous nations, where leaders are trying to extend access to
jobs to minorities hitherto locked out, they are utilizing various
devices that could be called preferences, quotas, "special measures" or set-asides. The objectives of affirmative action are somewhat different in various nations. In Peru, affirmative action is
directed at enhancing the economic and educational status of
Indians, who constitute the vast majority of the population. In
India, affirmative action is targeted at 22 percent of the population consisting of castes, the best known of which are the un-
touchables. In Israel, affirmative action has been justified as a
means of building the self-respect of groups, both Jews and
Arabs, who are held in low esteem.

It is significant that in the new Canadian constitution there is
an acceptance of affirmative action since the document explicitly
recognizes "any law, program or activity that has as its object
the amelioration of conditions of disadvantaged individuals or
groups."

In a summary of the papers and of the discussion on which the
Rockefeller report is based, the negative aspects of affirmative

action are noted. Affirmative action, some feel, leads to low self-esteem of those who have been advanced pursuant to its use. Affirmative action may also, it is urged, benefit persons who were not personally victimized, at the expense of some who were not oppressors. It is also claimed that affirmative action can lead to economic inefficiency by placing unqualified persons in positions of responsibility.

Affirmative action has, nonetheless, the Rockefeller study concludes, "made a positive difference where other measures have failed." The potential abuses in affirmative action, however, were warned against by Jack Greenberg, former general counsel to the N.A.A.C.P. Legal Defense Fund, who spent 25 years advancing various forms of affirmative action; he likened affirmative action to a "powerful drug that must be used for a serious illness but should be employed carefully to minimize objections and facilitate the goals it seeks to advance."

The American Association for Affirmative Action, a group of administrators for colleges, corporations and government agencies, has the difficult task of increasing the number of minority employees while being careful not to dilute quality. They understandably like to point to the successes of affirmative action in the past. Medical schools, for example, in the 1960's had a minority enrollment of 2.6 percent; in the late 1970's that figure was up to 8.2 percent. In 1970, there were 4,084 black female bus drivers; in 1980, there were 22,652. In 1962, there were 750 black employees at I.B.M.; in 1980, there were 16,546. In 1970, there were 962 black psychologists; in 1980, there were 6,756.

These amazing changes have many causes, but the official proponents and administrators of affirmative action programs understandably like to think that their objectives and their efforts have been important, if not crucial, in these developments. But the nation's administrators of affirmative action are wondering whether the next 10 years will bring new protests, or will the present controversies die down and the solid achievements of affirmative action in the years 1964 to 1984 be resumed? The answer to those questions depends in part on the future position of the Civil Rights Division of the Justice Department. Many of the top lawyers who directed that unit in 1981 have left—almost always in passionate dissent from the policies of Assistant Attorney General William Bradford Reynolds. The institutional memory of the Civil Rights Division may have been seriously damaged.

The future of affirmative action obviously also depends on what the courts decide in the next few months or years. But affirmative action probably depends more on the attitude that becomes dominant in American life during the balance of the 1980's. Up until the recent past, most individuals and corporations had welcomed affirmative action. It was a way to attract blacks into colleges and to places of employment. It was a reminder that women have been kept down in law firms, in industry and in higher education. And it taught a lesson that Hispanics had been discriminated against.

But now the consensus about affirmative action is less clear. An event in my class at Georgetown University Law Center revealed what a new generation is thinking about affirmative action.

Recently I put on the board for my class in constitutional law the median academic average and the scores on the law school admission test of the white and minority students at Georgetown Law Center. There is a difference of over 100 points between the scores of the white students and those of the minority. There is also a significant difference between the average grade quotient of these two types of students. Georgetown Law Center has 18 to 20 percent minority students—possibly the highest of any law school in the nation. The reactions of the class were very diverse. One black student said that she was "humiliated" that this information—routinely available to the faculty and to others—was publicized in this fashion. Another student asked if Georgetown, a Catholic institution, could use what he characterized as a "double standard" to increase or maintain the number of Catholics in the student body. A white student said with some anger that now he knew why his roommate at college was denied admission to Georgetown. One white student who identified himself as a Catholic said that he was proud of what Georgetown was doing but felt that it could possibly be struck down by a court.

The lack of a consensus among these 120 students, soon to be lawyers, reflects the deep division that exists almost everywhere regarding the thorny questions of affirmative action. Morris Abram, a noted civil rights attorney, does not make his position on affirmative action any clearer despite his continuous attempts to do so. Thomas Sowell, a black scholar sometimes identified with conservative groups, apparently feels that blacks will gradually emerge into the middle class just as the children and grandchildren of Germans, Italians and Scandinavians did. The vehemence demonstrated in the rejections of this position by civil rights attorneys and black leaders is an indication of the depths of feeling existing in those who feel that the concept of affirmative action is the only available way by which blacks and other minorities can be helped to reverse decades and decades of segregation and discrimination.

In almost every discussion of affirmative action, the unspoken question centers on the issue of whether "innocent" white people must somehow be required to pay a penalty because other white people discriminated on the basis of race. In 1976 the U.S. Supreme Court, while sustaining a form of affirmative action, approached this question with these words: "The result which we reach today . . . establishes that a sharing of the burden of the past discrimination is presumptively necessary."

Those opposed to affirmative action have the burden of offering an alternative that will advance the position of blacks, at least as much as affirmative action has done. To many people they do not appear to have sustained that burden. After all the arguments have been made and the controversies aired, the central reality comes back to the words of Justice Harry A. Blackmun, who in the Bakke decision wrote that "to get beyond racism we must first take account of race."

EDITOR'S INTRODUCTION

"The personal is political," a breezy catchphrase of the 1960s, contains a resonant truth. This section examines the impact of affirmative action on individual lives.

First, in "Victimized by Justice," Glen Hewitt, an unemployed professor sympathetic to affirmative action, writes of his own experience as a white male unable to secure a teaching position. Writing in *Christian Century,* Hewitt asserts that affirmative action is a "tragic choice, but a necessary one." The second article, "Affirmative Action: A New Form of Discrimination?" is by Henry Srebrnik, an unemployed Jewish academic who finds the racial categorization of people for employment to be "nonsensical."

In the following article, Ann F. Lewis rejects the conclusion of a study which claims that recipients of affirmative action are mentally tormented by the stigma. Whatever the stress, she says, "I never would have gotten in the door if other women hadn't organized to make sure some of us made it." Finally, Roger Wilkins in *Mother Jones* addresses black sensitivity to white resentment over affirmative action and points out that white people treated black people differently long before the advent of affirmative action. He advises black youngsters that "mental toughness and an independent sense of our own worth are elements as essential to the black survival kit in 1990 as they ever were."

VICTIMIZED BY JUSTICE[1]

Ours is a world of tragic choices. More often than not, there is no clear-cut right or wrong, no perfect answer to difficult dilemmas. The best we can do is to hurt fewer people rather than more, injure lightly rather than deeply. The soul gets grimy with compromise and calculation.

Such is the case with affirmative-action policies. No one having

[1]Reprint of an article by Glen A. Hewitt, religious studies scholar. Copyright 1987 Christian Century Foundation. Reprinted by permission from the September 23, 1987 issue of *The Christian Century.*

the least bit of intelligence and sensitivity can deny that women and minorities have been victimized by the gross injustices of overt and covert racism and sexism. One obvious response is to demand that such discrimination cease immediately, and to pass laws forbidding it. Such action is necessary and desirable. Though laws cannot change our inner prejudices, they can at least begin to prevent future injustices.

But what can be done to ameliorate the effects of past discrimination? To this there is no satisfactory answer. The pain and suffering of past generations—and of many people in the present one—cannot simply be erased. And yet there is something we can do. We can require for a time that the groups that have suffered discrimination be given preferential treatment in hiring and promotion. This requirement, in theory, will promote social justice by balancing the effects of discrimination among all social groups, even if discrimination is not eliminated entirely. This theory, affirmative action, is admittedly a compromise. It permits—in fact demands—injustice for a time so that a greater justice may be served. Ideally, the need for affirmative action will pass away, but the policy is necessary for a period in order to rectify—at least in part—past wrongs. Affirmative action is justified injustice. It is a tragic choice, but a necessary one.

Until recently, I had held all of the above as abstract truths which form an intrinsic part of an enlightened liberal world view. I still hold these truths, but they are no longer so abstract to me.

As a white, middle-class, male Protestant, I have never really experienced prejudice. But some years ago I felt called to the ministry of teaching religion in higher education. Gradually, I have come to experience the full force of affirmative action. After receiving a doctorate from one of the world's most renowned divinity schools, I could not get a job.

The advertisements for teaching positions all said "women and minorities especially encouraged to apply." It was the "especially" that was the kiss of death for white males. If women and minorities were only "encouraged" to apply, then it might be possible for a highly qualified white male to be seriously considered. But the "especially" removed all doubt. It was as if the ads read "White males need not apply." The dean of one university candidly admitted that he was looking for a black Catholic woman—and it wouldn't hurt if she were handicapped. Such dark humor has become a stock in trade for white males seeking teaching positions, just as such humor has served to ease some of the pain experienced by other groups.

In the past three years I have applied to more than 60 colleges and seminaries with advertised openings in my field, and have written letters of inquiry to 60 others. To date I have received only one offer; I accepted it and taught as a sabbatical replacement for one semester. Those who should know say my credentials are impeccable, and they are mystified at my lack of success. My white male friends, however, do understand.

I have no idea how many of the positions I applied for went to women or minorities, but I suspect that many did. That is good. Affirmative action is a policy I continue to support. But my particular interest here is not in those who have been victimized by injustice. My concern here is with those who are victimized by *justice*—namely, white males and their families.

There are many white males, well qualified to teach undergraduate and graduate courses, who are depressed and frustrated. They feel shut out of the academic job market. Though jobs are few and highly qualified applicants are plentiful, affirmative action is undoubtedly a major factor in academic hiring. Most administrators will readily admit as much. But prejudicial hiring, even when justified, takes on a different tone when it victimizes me.

I suffer two great pains in my situation. First, I am denied the opportunity to exercise my ministry, to which I believe God has called me, and for which I spent nine years in preparation. Second, I must watch my family suffer.

Recently I received another rejection. The news came by phone. I had been very optimistic about this job; I had connections at the school. I knew every member of the department. They had asked me to apply. I had had a very comfortable preliminary interview with them. But they had hired a woman. I have no doubt that she is well qualified for the position—perhaps more so than I. She is a graduate of a leading divinity school. She has expertise in this field. Despite my great disappointment, I can understand and approve of the department's decision.

When I got off the phone and told my wife, she burst into tears. How ironic that she too should suffer from the justice of affirmative action. She has labored for nearly ten years, supporting me while I pursued my dream. She is an overworked, underpaid, underappreciated elementary school teacher. She has put her dreams for a house and family on hold for ten years—willingly—for my dream was her dream, too. And now she is denied her dream.

I am obviously not the first to experience these pains; there have always been "in" groups and "out" groups. But my pain is real. It hurts to see a loved one cry. It hurts to feel doors to a career closed before they have opened. It hurts to be unable to respond to a clear-cut call to ministry.

Affirmative action is working. Women and minorities are making some slow gains. But there is danger that we (mostly white males) who are victims of justice will find our pain fueling anger, hostility and latent prejudices. Instead, we should use it to become "wounded healers," helping to rescue others from the pain and injustice of discrimination. We must allow our pain to sensitize us to others' pain.

In my case, that means renewing my support for women and minorities in the ministry. I belong to a denomination in which women are scarcely ever allowed to be pastors. That is horribly unjust; there is absolutely no biblical warrant for it. I must recommit myself to opposing that discrimination actively.

Perhaps the day will come when affirmative action is no longer necessary. Perhaps then job applicants will be judged not by race or sex, but solely by professional qualifications.

AFFIRMATIVE ACTION: A NEW FORM OF DISCRIMINATION?[2]

Drop in at any university faculty lounge, where academics engage in casual "shop talk"—or better yet, attend a hiring committee meeting selecting candidates for a teaching job. You will find the conversation is primarily not about qualifications, but gender and race. Except that the hiring priorities are reversed, you might think you were back in the old South—or South Africa. Though some pretend otherwise, hiring is now done on the basis of informal quotas. That's the way chairs and administrators keep score.

First off, let me state my personal interest. I am a "white male" in his 40s, with a Ph.D. in political science, who for years has been unable to obtain a tenure-track academic position (though I

[2]Reprint of an article by Henry Srebrnik, professor of political science, University of Calgary. *Jewish Currents* 44:7–11, October 1990. Reprinted with permission.

taught for nine years at a Canadian college). I don't claim to be anything special, either as a scholar or teacher (though I am told I have good letters attesting to my talents in both areas), nor are my degrees from Ivy League universities (though they are all from well-regarded schools).

Yet, despite the tight job market and any deficiencies I might have as an academic, I know from personal observation and a wealth of anecdotal evidence that, were I either a Black male or a white woman (even one middle-aged) with the same credentials, I would have managed to obtain a position at some college somewhere. I lose out to people simply on the basis of unalterable and irreducible biological attributes such as sex and skin color—which neither political "consciousness raising" nor cultural transformation can change. I know I speak for many "white males" who feel as I do—but are afraid to contradict today's "party line."

Feminists will be outraged to think that their philosophy can in any way be compared (not equated, simply compared) with such odious ideologies as Nazism. But let's look at them both. I'm willing to grant one major difference: Nazi race theories were lunacy, in that the contradistinction between the superior "Aryan" and the subhuman "Jew" was myth gone mad, whereas, clearly, there are genuine physical categories such as men and women.

However, once we accept this admittedly important distinction, are they in some ways similar? Both ideologies relate to people as irreducible "physical" categories that are, in the end, immutable. Not every German was a Nazi, of course; but for Nazism, Germans as a category (even those who were "misguided" enough not to appreciate it) were by definition superior to others. A Jew, on the other hand, even if he could have convinced himself that Hitler was correct, was by racial definition an *untermensch*, hence not eligible for entry into the Aryan family.

I personally have always probably been a "feminist," long before the word was coined. As a child, I was bad at sports, and didn't "hang around with the guys." Football, hunting and all of the madness associated with "male culture" are repugnant to me. "Feminine" values have always been more attractive.

But if I did pass this ideological means test, does this make me a feminist? Even if it did, would feminists think I ought to have an advantage when it came to academic jobs? Or would they still prefer a woman, even one still laboring under "false consciousness" and hence not feminist in her ideals and teaching? I think we know the answer. In the end, it's a physical matter.

(Marxism, on the other hand, does allow for class transformations. Even a Rockefeller can, theoretically, become a Marxist—and no one would then say it still isn't good enough because she's not the actual daughter of workers.)

But feminism is more than zoological. It is also reactionary. Its objective effect is to remove men increasingly from the humanistic spheres—"everyone" will tell you, in a frank moment, that it would be career suicide for a man today to do a Ph.D. in disciplines such as history, English or sociology.

What will be the effect on our society, though, when high school and college boys, knowing they have no chance for employment if they enter these disciplines, are forced by the marketplace into law, business, engineering—and the military? I happen to believe men are, for a complex variety of cultural and historical reasons, more aggressive and vicious than are women. Is it really a step forward to force men into fields that will only reinforce their already aggressive and competitive behavior, while college teaching becomes—like nursing and schoolteaching before it—a "caring" profession in the hands of "schoolmarms"?

Apart from being racist and reactionary, feminism is divisive. Clearly, it is men such as myself—people on the left, humanists, etc.—who are most likely to be sympathetic to the women's movement, but not, finally, at the cost of being unemployed in a capitalist society where being without work is an incredibly frightening experience for those of non-elite backgrounds. Generals, police, stockbrokers and others less affected will, ironically, be able to pay lip service to feminist ideals without worrying about the consequences. But men aspiring to be scholars will increasingly find their selfish motives overriding their idealism.

I present three examples to make by point: At one school, a history department had just lost a young woman to a major university. As it was too late to advertise a tenure-track position, they hired a one-year replacement. The successful candidate was a white male in his late 30s with a Ph.D. from a Big Ten university. He had been living this kind of "gypsy" existence for years, going from one job to the next. When I asked the woman he was replacing whether her former department might consider hiring him a year later for the tenure-track position, she replied, "Oh, no, they must hire a woman."

At this same college, another department advertising a tenure-track position interviewed three candidates: a white man, a white woman and a Black woman. A member of the department told me privately that the male candidate was, in terms of credentials and merit, clearly the best candidate, with the white woman second and the Black woman third. However, the offers would be made in the reverse order.

This same school has faculty members who feel that any Black or woman who meets minimal qualifications for a position ought to be hired for the position. The academic dean of the college has announced that a white male would have to be "visibly superior" (a criterion that in fact goes beyond the laws governing affirmative action).

What makes this whole scenario even more delicious are the ironies involved: one white male who didn't get a permanent job at this school was himself a Marxist whose academic interests and methodology were far to the left of a Black candidate he competed with. But, as one woman faculty member (herself a radical lesbian) said, "As far as the administration is concerned, it has to be a Black, and it wouldn't matter if it was Duvalier."

Here's an even better example—indeed, as controlled an experiment as one can get in the real world: I know of a couple who are both Africanists. The man is an established scholar with a book published by an Ivy League press, and has been the recipient of prestigious postdoctoral grants. He has, nonetheless, been unable to find a job. His wife, who only recently defended her Ph.D. thesis, has already been offered a tenure-track position.

In less enlightened times, businesses posted signs saying "No Irish Need Apply," and restrictions against Jews were considered "normal." Today, in universities, it is considered proper to feel that "white males" should be hired only as a last resort.

In any case, not only do I object to classifying people in nonvoluntary collective categories, but I find the very categories nonsensical (this is why I have put the term "white male" in quotes). As a child of Polish Jewish Holocaust survivors who grew up within the English-speaking minority in French-majority Quebec, the last thing I ever considered myself was a "white male"—nor, I very strongly suspect, did any of the Montreal WASP elite or French Canadians, male or female, who in those days certainly looked down upon immigrant Jews. Immense ethnic, cultural and religious differences—differences that, in Europe and elsewhere, were the very causes of wars!—are all subsumed under the rubric "white male." It boggles the mind.

So there is an element of sheer absurdity, as well as pain, in all of this for me. To be told I am a "white male" and hence privileged—when 30 years ago some of these very people might have discriminated against me as a lower-class Jew—truly angers me.

These categories make no sense for others as well. Is a coal miner's son from Appalachia, perhaps the first person in his family to have gone to university and then obtained a doctorate from a state university, really more disadvantaged than an upper-class woman with a Ph.D. from Yale, whose mother might have attended Wellesley? Who should be eligible for affirmative action in this case? In actuality, though, the job competition would more likely be between this woman and her male cousin, as it were, with a Harvard Ph.D. The feminization of faculties thus rarely changes their class composition. They remain overwhelmingly the preserve of the upper middle classes.

The growth of a class of professional women has simply replicated among women the patterns of hierarchy and divisions of labor already found among men. Today, we have an increasing female army of low-paid daycare workers, maids, nannies and babysitters (most often non-white or lower class), working for upwardly mobile women. (If surrogate motherhood ever does become acceptable, they will also end up bearing the children—truly liberating bourgeois women into becoming bourgeois men's equals.) So, slogans about "sisterhood" notwithstanding, one effect of feminism has been to widen class gaps among women. For women doing domestic chores for other women, being told men are the primary source of oppression must ring hollow indeed.

But perhaps feminism and like-minded ideologies—despite their own self-perception as being leftwing—are in fact profoundly anti-socialist. After all, to categorize people as women, Blacks, Hispanics, etc. is simply a new way of denying that class is what matters. (How incredible all this would be to some Rip van Winkle who had fallen asleep in the 1930s. Then, it was reactionaries and segregationists who tried to divide workers along racial lines!) It would be harder to carry this off in countries with a history of class consciousness: try telling an East London cockney that he and the Duke of Bedford, as "white males," are both somehow equally more privileged than, say, Lady Churchill.

The gender division is not the only one that obfuscates and confuses real class and ethnic differences. The Hispanic label, too, can theoretically lead to ludicrous situations: does it refer only to Latin Americans? Or is the Duke of Alba, too, a Hispanic?

If it includes European Latins, then why not also Italians or French? Is a Jew from Argentina Hispanic? If not, then does it really mean a "Christian" or non-white?

As for the category "Black," does it include anyone with darker skin—say, a Sikh, an Ethiopian Jew, a Bengali or even a Berber? If not, why not? I am familiar with one small liberal arts college where more than half the Black faculty are Africans who are now U.S. citizens. They tend to be from their respective nations' elites. How does such hiring (which statistically adheres to affirmative action goals) help those whom it was meant to help—historically disadvantaged American Blacks?

Will the U.S. eventually become some new type of multi-national state, as the Austro-Hungarian and Ottoman Empires were, with different national minorities (now also subdivided by gender) jostling for jobs? We should be wary of this new form of communalism, which will result in a society with no common political ethos. One needs only look at places like Cyprus or Lebanon to see where it could lead.

Of course all this is begging the ultimate question: is the fact that any given group in society (no matter how defined) is not perfectly represented, statistically, in any given profession a sign of discrimination? We all know Jews are vastly overrepresented in academia—yet not only were they not given any special advantages by those running the universities, attempts were made to keep them out for many decades. On the other hand, Jews are incredibly underrepresented in professional sports. Is this a matter of discrimination? Should teams make efforts to recruit Jews (perhaps even at the expense of more qualified players from other groups) simply so that teams may reflect the composition of the population at large (or at least the spectators)? Why does this sound any more ludicrous than what is happening in universities?

As a Jew, I see a final piece of irony in all of this: I'm sure I'm not revealing any secrets to anyone reading this article when I mention that Jews have been vastly overrepresented in another category: people on the left. As revolutionaries and socialists, Jews have consistently fought on behalf of other people. But at least they expected that, in a more enlightened society, they would have the same rights as everyone else. Now, in the U.S., the many Jewish males who were active in the civil rights movement, SDS, the New Left, etc., have in effect been told—by many who claim to be radicals—that they are part of the privileged "enemy."

History truly does play jokes on people.

THANKS GUYS: WE'LL TAKE
AFFIRMATIVE ACTION, ANYWAY[3]

I was reading the *Wall Street Journal* one morning, trying once again to figure out the difference between corrupt illegal insider trading and regular well-informed business practices, when I realized the front page of the *Journal* was directed at me.

Yes, there it was, in the space usually reserved for major business developments and other news for the deserving rich: the truth about affirmative action.

Many Minorities Feel Torn by Experience of Affirmative Action, the headline read. *While Program Opens Doors, It Can Attach a Stigma That Affects Self-Esteem.*

And all this time we were worried about discrimination! While we were foolishly concerned with such minor issues as getting good jobs and the salaries that go with them, those diligent researchers at the National Institute of Conventional Wisdom have been hard at work. They have uncovered the true threat to the well-being of women and minorities: the stigma of affirmative action.

This explanation should certainly make us feel better about recent Supreme Court decisions. Those misleading news reports made it sound as if we were losing protection when the Court narrowed the scope of affirmative action programs and civil rights legislation. Now we learn they were just trying to save our self-esteem.

Friends, I am not making this up. A whole series of pundits have arrived at the same conclusion, expressed in the latest, pseudo-scientific jargon: "The psychic cost of affirmative action . . . is very high," says TRB in *The New Republic* magazine, ". . . as high, psychologically, as segregation was." The author of these comments is absolutely objective: he has had no personal experience with either.

By denying recognition of the underrepresented and the underemployed, opponents of affirmative action are helping us preserve the thrill that comes from trying to make it in the real world—their world—without help. Also without being part of the

[3]Reprint of an article by Ann F. Lewis, national affairs columnist, *Ms.* 18:86, September 1989. *Ms.* Copyright September 1989. Reprinted with permission.

old boys' network, without mentors, recommendations, or the
contacts made on the golf course . . . it's a thrill a minute out
there. And good for us, besides.

Sound familiar? This advice is being given to us for OUR
OWN GOOD, and someday we'll be grateful. It's part of that
series of patronizing homilies: *Advice to women from people who are
smarter than we are.*

Remember some of the previous entries in this category: how
college education would shrink a woman's uterus; and—most recently—success in business would give us heart attacks.

The astute reader will have noticed that neither of these dire
predictions ever came true. The latest reports show that successful women are actually healthier than women in lower paid,
higher stress jobs. And I believe we can cope with the stress of
affirmative action too. In fact, I know we can.

You see, I was an affirmative action hire myself. When I was
selected as political director of the Democratic National Committee in 1981, it was understood that the party needed to have
women in high-ranking, visible jobs.

I was a good political director, a job that carries a significant
amount of stress. But no one would have known how good I was
if I hadn't gotten in the door. And I never would have gotten in
the door if other women hadn't organized to make sure some of
us made it.

So thanks for the advice, fellows—but no thanks. We're prepared to take our chances with affirmative action—especially because we understand what the alternative would be. And if you're
really concerned with our psychic well-being, take some advice
from women for a change: join us in a coalition that works to keep
the doors open for everybody.

IN IVORY TOWERS[4]

Blacks are among those expressing second thoughts about
affirmative action in college and university life these days. The
first concern is expressed by a brilliant young black friend, who

[4]Article by Roger Wilkins, civil rights activist. From *Mother Jones,* Copyright 1990
Foundation for National Progress. Reprinted with permission.

laments that despite his formidable intellectual accomplishments, people still judge him not as a splendid scholar, but only as a smart black. The second is a concern expressed by some black educators that students admitted under affirmative action programs may come to doubt their own capacities as a result.

These complaints proceed from the same idea: that the main thing to think about when considering affirmative action is the damage it does to black self-esteem—either because whites will doubt blacks' capacities, or because the remedy itself makes blacks doubt their own capacities. I understand this burden, having carried part of it all my adult life, but the simple colloquial response I give to black faculty members and black students who express similar concerns to me is: "You're upset because you think *affirmative action* makes white folks look at you funny. Hell, white folks were looking at black folks funny long before affirmative action was invented. They been lookin' at black folks funny since 1619."

The founding tenet of racism is that blacks are inferior, particularly when it comes to intellectual capability. And an underpinning of racism has been an all-out cultural onslaught on the self-esteem of blacks, to transform them from assertive and self-sufficient human beings into dependents, mere extensions of the will of the whites who choose to use them.

Affirmative action, even weakly and spottily deployed, opens doors of opportunity that would otherwise be slammed tight. As a result, the country is better and stronger. It surely is one of the most effective antidotes to the widespread habit of undervaluing the capacities of minorities and women. It also serves as a counterbalance to the tendency to overvalue, as a recruitment tool, the effectiveness and fairness of old-boy networks.

But affirmative action did not magically erase racism. It simply pushed back the boundaries of the struggle a little bit, giving some of us better opportunities to fulfill our capacities, and higher perches from which to conduct our battles. Anyone who thinks there are no more battles to be fought, even on the highest battlements of the ivoriest of the ivory towers, simply doesn't understand America.

Whatever confusion I've had about such things was knocked out of me a long time ago. Almost everything that has happened to me since I was twenty-one has resulted from one sort of affirmative action or another. Thirty-seven years as the object of affirmative action in such places as the Department of Justice, the Ford Foundation, the *Washington Post* and the *New York Times* have given me a rich understanding of the endurance of U.S. racism. I have done battle and emerged with enough self-confidence to assert that all of the places that hired me because of affirmative action were better for having done so.

Nevertheless, I am sympathetic to the desire of my young black friend for the excellence of his mind to wash the color off his accomplishments. Unfortunately, even in 1990, color is not irrelevant in the United States at any level—and perhaps that is fortunate, for it maintains some fragmentary bond between my friend and poor black people who need his concern and strength. I am reminded, in this regard, of the wisdom embedded in an old joke that comes from deep in African-American culture. In this story, two old white men are rocking on a porch in a Southern town. Says the first, "Zeke, what do you call a black man with a Ph.D. who has just won the Nobel Prize in physics?" Replies Zeke, after a long pause and much contemplative rocking, "I calls him nigger."

Not all white people are as deeply racist as Zeke, of course, but enough are to make it wise for young black people to follow what our mothers and fathers have taught us over the generations: that white people's judgments of us are to be viewed with great skepticism, and that accepting those judgments whole is apt to be hazardous to our mental health. Thus, mental toughness and an independent sense of our own worth are elements as essential to the black survival kit in 1990 as they ever were.

Not only do black professors need to know this, but black students entering predominantly white campuses have to be taught it, as well. Such campuses are products of white-American culture, and most black youngsters, particularly those from the inner cities, find them to be alien places. Moreover, they sometimes get mixed messages. Often recruited assiduously, they frequently find pockets of hostility and seas of indifference.

That is not a reason for less affirmative action, but for more—at the faculty, staff level. There should be many black adults on those campuses to make them feel less foreign to black students and more like places of opportunity, full of challenges that can be overcome with excellence and effort. If the number of knowledgeable and sympathetic adults is minuscule, the youngsters will see that the commitment to an atmosphere where everyone can learn is crimped and limited.

In this imperfect world, racism remains a major affliction that burdens all Americans—and it hits black Americans right in the self-esteem. But it must surely be easier to firm up your self-regard when you are employed with tenure than when working as an itinerant researcher. Similarly, the task is undoubtedly easier for a college graduate—even one who had to struggle with self-doubt during college years because of affirmative action—than for someone who has never gone to college.

It would be nice to think that in the academy we could escape cultural habits wrought during more than three centuries of legal racial oppression. But that won't happen in this century. So black people—even those who are privileged—just have to suck it in and keep on pushing, breaking their own paths and making a way for those still struggling behind.

BIBLIOGRAPHY

An asterisk (*) preceding a reference indicates that the article or part of it has been reprinted in this book.

BOOKS AND PAMPHLETS

Bell, Derrick A. And we are not saved: the elusive quest for racial justice. Basic Books. '87.

Belz, Herman. Equality transformed: a quarter century of affirmative action. Social Philosophy and Policy Center, Transaction Publishers. '90.

Blanchard, Fletcher A. and Crosby, Faye, eds. Affirmative action in perspective. Springer-Verlag. '89.

Capaldi, Nicholas. Out of order: affirmative action and the crisis of doctrinaire liberalism. Prometheus Books. '85.

Davis, George and Watson Glegg. Black life in corporate America: swimming in the mainstream. Anchor Press/Doubleday. '82.

Dex, Shirley and Shaw, Lois Banfill. British and American women at work: do equal opportunity policies matter? St. Martin's Press. '86.

Feagin, Joe R. and Clairece Booher. Discrimination American style: institutional racism and sexism. Krieger. '86.

Fear, Richard A. and Ross, James F. Jobs, dollars and EEO: how to hire more productive entry-level workers. McGraw-Hill. '83.

Glazer, Nathan. Affirmative discrimination: ethnic inequality and public policy. Harvard University Press. '87.

Greene, Kathanne W. Affirmative action and principles of justice. Greenwood Press. '89.

Kellough, Edward J. Federal equal employment opportunity policy and numerical goals and timetables: an impact assessment. Praeger. '89.

Lynch, Frederick R. Invisible victims: white males and the crisis of affirmative action. Greenwood Press. '89.

Nieli, Russell. Racial preference and racial justice: the new affirmative action controversy. Ethics and Public Policy Center. '90.

O'Neill, Timothy J. Bakke and the politics of equality: friends and foes in the classroom of litigation. Wesleyan University Press. '85.

Rosenfeld, Michel. Affirmative action and justice: a philosophical and constitutional inquiry. Yale University Press. '91.

Schwartz, Bernard. Behind Bakke: affirmative action and the supreme court. New York University Press. '88.

Shulman, Steven, Darity, William A. and Higgs, Robert. The question of discrimination: racial inequality in the US labor market. Wesleyan University Press. '89.

Therstrom, Abigail M. Whose votes count?: affirmative action and minority voting rights. Harvard University Press. '87.

Urofsky, Melvin I. A conflict of rights; the Supreme Court and affirmative action. Scribner's Sons, Collier Macmillan. '91.

Wallace, Phyllis Ann, ed. Women in the workplace. Auburn House. '82.

Witherspoon, Floyd. Equal employment and affirmative action: a source book. Garland. '85.

Witt, Stephanie L. The pursuit of race and gender equity in American academe. Praeger. '90.

Woods, Geraldine. Affirmative action. Watts. '89.

Work, John W. Toward affirmative action and racial/ethnic pluralism: how to train in organization, a handbook for trainers. Belvedere Press. '89.

Wyzan, Michael L., ed. The political economy of ethnic discrimination and affirmative action: a comparative perspective. Praeger Publishers. '90.

ADDITIONAL PERIODICAL ARTICLES WITH ABSTRACTS

For those who wish to read more widely on the subject of affirmative action, this section contains abstracts of additional articles that bear on the topic. Readers who require a comprehensive list of materials are advised to consult the Readers' Guide to Periodical Literature and other Wilson indexes.

LEGAL DIMENSION TO AFFIRMATIVE ACTION

Constitutional crisis (Supreme Court rulings on employment discrimination). Peggy Simpson *Ms. Magazine* 18:90+ S '89

The 1989 session of the Supreme Court dealt a series of devastating defeats to women and minority men, confirming that the Reagan Revolution has taken root in the Court. As a result of the session's rulings, women and minorities will find it extremely difficult to prove discrimination, and they will have little recourse against subtle barriers to hiring and career advancement. Many affirmative actions programs may legally be abandoned, and some may even be made unlawful. Civil rights activists hope to minimize the damage by scrutinizing future judicial appointments and carefully monitoring George Bush's plan to revamp the Commission on Civil Rights. A sidebar outlines major civil rights rulings of the 1989 Supreme Court session.

Birmingham firehouse (Supreme Court decision permitting white firemen to bring suit against the city for job discrimination). *Commonweal* 116:387–8 Jl 14 '89

The Supreme Court's decision in Martin v. Wilks marks a retreat from the use of affirmative action agreements as a rough gauge of fairness. In 1981, the city government of Birmingham, Alabama, signed a consent decree to hire and promote blacks in the municipal fire department. In Martin v. Wilks, the majority of the Court allowed white firemen to sue the city because the consent decree discriminated against them. The Court has thus ruled that affirmative action agreements, even court-approved ones, are subject to countercharges of discrimination. Members of Congress have promised remedial legislation. Nevertheless, the decision may permit interminable legal challenges to affirmative action consent decrees which could ultimately discourage blacks and civil rights organizations from defending the decrees.

What have they done for us lately? (Supreme Court and affirmative action). Linda Villarosa *Essence* 21:66+ My '90

The future of affirmative action is at risk. In the past 20 years, affirmative action has helped increase the number of black-owned businesses, black lawyers, and black managers/administrators. In 1989, however, the Reagan-influenced Supreme Court made several rulings that eroded the equal-opportunity gains made during the past 20 years, posing a threat to the economic health of women and people of color. With or without government support, the black community must work to hold onto the gains of the past two decades and to expand them by building up its own businesses, speaking out against discrimination, striving for education, and keeping its dollars in the black community.

A blow to affirmative action (Supreme Court strikes down Richmond, Va. minority set-aside law. Andrea Sachs *Time* 133:60 F 6 '89

Affirmative action recently suffered a setback when the Supreme Court struck down a Richmond, Virginia, ordinance designed to guarantee minorities a greater share of the city's construction contracts. Writing for the majority, Justice Sandra Day O'Connor argued that the city had not specifically proved a level of past discrimination that would justify its law, which set aside 30 percent of the dollar amount of its municipal projects for minority-owned construction firms. The requirement that all government distinctions based on race be subject to strict scrutiny was a key component of the decision. The ruling, which three dissenting justices decried as a giant step backward, jeopardizes similar programs in other states and may lead to legal attacks on other racially based government schemes. It does not affect plans by private companies to increase minority hiring, however, and it leaves the federal government's set-aside program intact.

Civil rights cases (Supreme Court) *Monthly Labor Review* 112:50–1 Ag '89

The U.S. Supreme Court issued four rulings that were widely perceived to hinder the efforts of women and minorities seeking to redress allegedly unfair employment practices. In Wards Cove Packing Company v. Antonio, the Court ruled that employees must prove that racial imbalances in their employers' work forces are the result of practices with no business justification. In Martin v. Wilks, the right of a group of white firefighters in Birmingham, Alabama, to challenge a court-ordered affirmative action plan was upheld. In Lorance v. AT&T Technologies, the Court held that three women employees waited too long before filing a lawsuit charging the company with sexual discrimination.

Supreme Court set aside ruling not devastating blow to black businesses. *Jet* 75:4 F 13 '89

The Supreme Court has struck down a Richmond, Virginia ordinance requiring that a percentage of construction contracts be awarded to minority businesses. United States Supreme Court justice Thurgood Marshall who authored the dissenting opinion, called the decision a deliberate and giant step backward for affirmative action in the United States. According to National Minority Business Council president John F. Robinson, however, the ruling should not be a devastating blow to black businesses, as only one-eighth of minority businesses participate in such programs.

AFFIRMATIVE ACTION PROSPECTS IN THE NEW MILLENNIUM

A tenuous bond from 9 to 5 (blacks working for IBM) Barbara Kantrowitz *Newsweek* 111:24–5 Mr 7 '88

Part of a cover story on relations between blacks and whites in America. The success of corporate affirmative-action programs has been mixed. Many blacks feel that they must work twice as hard as whites to be considered equal and that their achievements are regarded as race-based. The wage gap between blacks and whites has increased slightly, and there are still few blacks in many professions. Many companies have worked to encourage understanding and friendship between blacks and whites, however. IBM has a decades-old commitment to equal opportunity. It recruits aggressively at black colleges, reviews its equal opportunity policy annually, has well-defined grievance policies, and supports its employees outside the workplace.

The blow to affirmative action may not hurt that much (Supreme Court) Paula Dwyer *Business Week* 61–2 Jl 3 '89

Reflecting a new conservative majority, the Supreme Court has issued a series of rulings that make it more difficult for women and minorities to redress complaints of discrimination in the workplace. The decisions have addressed highly technical points of law, but taken together they represent a fundamental reshaping of civil rights laws. They won't necessarily lead to a conservative revolution in the workplace, however. Women, minorities, and immigrants will make up 80 percent of the growth in the labor force by the year 2000, forcing companies to have active outreach programs to remain competitive. A sidebar summarizes the five cases that changed the rules.

Holding firm on affirmative action (Fortune poll) Alan Farnham
Fortune 119:87–8 Mr 13 '89

The results of a recent Fortune 500/CNN Moneyline poll reveal chief executive officers' thoughts on affirmative-action programs. Despite statistics that indicate the relative failure of affirmative-action programs, and despite the Supreme Court's recent ruling against a set-aside law in Richmond, Virginia, 42 percent of the poll's respondents say that they are still fully committed to affirmative action, and 59 percent say that they do not intend to change their established programs. Their support stems from a mixture of social consciousness, fear of penalties, and smart business. By the end of the 1990s, 85 percent of new employees will be women or black, Hispanic, or Asian men. In recent months, however, executives' support of affirmative action has not guaranteed minority employees' jobs. Corporate restructuring and the stock market crash have led to massive layoffs. Since minorities are often the last hired, they are also among the first fired.

Get ready for the new workforce. Joel Dreyfus *Fortune* 121:165+
Ap 23, '90

As annual work force growth slows in the 1990s, U.S. companies that tap the growing segments of the labor market—women and minorities—will succeed. To ease the way for these workers, firms are creating literacy programs, instituting flexible work schedules, and providing child care. They are also training staff to be more tolerant of language and cultural differences, to reject racial and sexual prejudices, and to be more accommodating to the handicapped.

Black executives: how they're doing. Colin Leinster *Fortune*
117:109–10+ Ja 18 '88

The progress of blacks in corporate America has been disappointing. There is only one black chairman and chief executive within the Fortune 1000, and a 1986 survey showed that less than 9 percent of all managers are minorities. Many factors have contributed to this situation: Not enough blacks have the degrees in business administration, engineering, and hard science that businesses needed, so blacks have often been hired to fill staff positions—the first to be eliminated in restructuring. Affirmative action has not worked, and the Reagan administration's lack of interest in it has been imitated by companies. Most blacks view discrimination as a fact of life in the workplace, but the most successful blacks are those who worked hard and pressed ahead despite discrimination.

Atlanta: keeping affirmative action alive. Kevin D. Thompson
Black Enterprise 20:48 S '89

The Georgia supreme court established tougher guidelines for minority set-aside programs in March, and the city of Atlanta is now working to preserve its program, Minority Business Enterprise. Two economic consultants have been commissioned to compile and analyze statistical and anecdotal information that is expected to illustrate how racial discrimination has limited the ability of women and minorities to compete for government contracts. Mayor Andrew Young will review the study when it is completed in October and then decide whether Atlanta will devise a new set-aside program in accordance with the court-imposed standards. Similar studies may soon be conducted in Tampa, Milwaukee, and Denver.

Affirmative action in vogue? Mark A. Fortune *Black Enterprise* 19:20 Ap '89

According to a Labor Department study entitled Opportunity 2000, women and minorities are becoming increasingly marketable because employers face a shrinking pool of employable workers. The study reports that by the year 2000, 75 percent of all available workers will be women, minorities, and immigrants. Employers are responding by increasing their recruitment, education, and training of women, ethnic minorities, and disabled and older workers.

HIGHER EDUCATION

Beyond affirmative action: empowering Asian American faculty. Sucheng Chan *Change* 21:48–51 N/D '89

Part of a special issue on Asian Americans and education. Asian Americans must work to become more involved in every sector of a university's structure. To gain an understanding of the nature of a university and the roles that its different members play, more Asian Americans must be willing to do committee work. They should also strive to enter administrative and key staff positions. Meanwhile, they should work to develop better interpersonal skills and build public pressure to improve their situation.

Quotas on campus: the new phase (Asian American students). Daniel Seligman *Fortune* 119:205+ Ja 30 '89

U.S. Department of Education investigations into the possibility that some colleges are discriminating against Asian Americans point up problems in the logic of affirmative action. In 1978, the Supreme Court's Bakke decision legitimized preference for minorities in college admissions, and Asian students were among those targeted for affirmative action. In the 1980s, however, preference for Asian American students has turned into an embarrassment in light of Asians' economic success and their growing numbers in the student bodies of top-flight schools. In the language of affirmative action, Asian Americans have become overrepresented on campus and should therefore suffer reverse discrimination, much like whites. Even affirmative action advocates, however, question the logic of restricting Asians if they represent the best and ablest students.

The alarming decline in the number of black college students.
Marilyn Marshall *Ebony* 42:44+ S '87

The number of blacks, particularly males, enrolling in U.S. colleges has been steadily declining since 1976, the year black college enrollment peaked. Experts list several factors for the decline, including escalating college costs, federal student aid cutbacks, a deemphasis on affirmative action, and often hostile environments on predominantly white campuses. The decrease in the number of black male college students is attributed to mounting socioeconomic pressure, drug abuse, incarceration, and entrance into the military. Suggestions from black educators on reversing the enrollment decline are provided.

Blacks in higher education: the climb toward equality. *Change* 19:6–7+ My/Je '87

A special issue examines the status of blacks in the mainstream of U.S. higher education. The movement of the 1960s and 1970s to bring blacks into higher education has fizzled. Questions that were raised at that time are still unanswered, including whether the efforts to integrate white schools should focus on parity or standards and whether historically black institutions are anachronisms or are destined to come into their own. The situation is made more complex by a deteriorating racial climate that is characterized by impatience with remedial programs, distaste for affirmative action, and sharpened debate over meritocracy and equity. It is time to renew efforts to make the black presence in higher education more pervasive and more significant.

Missing element: Hispanics at the top in higher education.
Leonard Valverde *Change* 20:11 My/Je '88

Part of an issue on Hispanics in higher education. After 20 years of affirmative action, it is still rare for Hispanics to be appointed to chief executive positions in higher education. The few colleges and universities that have succeeded in creating equal opportunity for Hispanic populations are headed by Hispanic presidents and chancellors committed to minority attainment. Leaders must commit themselves to include Hispanic academics in executive positions, take steps to prepare Hispanics for executive roles, and foster the executive potential of talented Hispanics.

Admitting success (discussion of December 31, 1984 article, affirmative racism). Charles A. Murray *The New Republic* 192:14–16 F 4 '85

The author responds to an article calling affirmative action in higher education racist and ineffectual (December 31, 1984) by pointing to the advantages of such policies. Critics say preferential admissions fuel white prejudice and that without them blacks would eventually struggle to success the way other ethnic groups have done in America. But studies have shown that most white students never question the abilities of their black peers. Some schools and black students could work harder to raise the academic performance of disadvantaged entrants, but test scores as a criterion for acceptance must be balanced by consideration of the benefits of white and blacks learning together. The nonpreferential approach of years past, the only alternative offered by critics, has helped few blacks attain the professional status that begins to repair the injustices of slavery and encourage future generations.

Separate but equal all over again (Louisiana public colleges fight desegregation order). Thomas Toch *U.S. News & World Report* 108:37+ Ap 23 '90

A federal court in New Orleans has ordered Louisiana, where public higher education is largely segregated, to eliminate the racial identifiability of its 19 colleges and universities. Enrollment is at least 90 percent black at 4 state schools and 74 to 92 percent white at 14 others. The court called for the merging of the Louisiana State University and Southern University law schools and of the governing boards of the state's three university systems. It also required racial enrollment ceilings and affirmative action admissions policies at all state schools. The Citizens' Committee for Equity and Excellence in Louisiana's Universities and the state chapter of the NAACP say that the plan doesn't go far enough toward desegregation, but the 4 black colleges and many black educators want to keep things as they are because the black schools serve students who are shunned at other schools and are important sources of black social and political influence.

Affirmative action: the new look. Andrew Hacker *The New York Review of Books* 36:63–8 O 12 '89

In an essay on affirmative action in American education, the writer discusses the educational opportunities and achievements of various minorities and comments on eight books: Eliminating Racism: Profiles in Controversy, edited by Phyllis A. Katz and Dalmas A. Taylor; Freshman Admissions at Berkeley: A Policy for the 1990s and Beyond, a report by the admissions committee at the University of California-Berkeley; Choosing a College: A Guide for Parents and Students, by Thomas Sowell; The Case Against the SAT, by James Crouse and Dale Trusheim; Blacks in College: A Comparative Study of Students' Success in Black and in White Institutions, by Jacqueline Fleming; A Common Destiny: Blacks and American Society, edited by Gerald David Jaynes and Robin M. Williams, Jr.; Visions of a Better Way: A Black Appraisal of Public Schooling, by the Committee on Policy for Racial Justice; and Minorities in Higher Education, edited by Reginald Wilson and Deborah J. Carter.

The undergraduate Hispanic experience: a case of juggling two cultures. Edward B. Fiske *Change* 20:28–33 My/Je '88

Part of an issue on Hispanics in higher education. Hispanic students often face profound culture shock when they enter college. Their sense of alienation may be compounded by curricula that rarely reflect Hispanic interests. They find it difficult to break family ties that are an essential part of their culture, and they lack role models and adequate support systems. Hispanic students who are supported by affirmative action programs may feel obliged to prove their worth. They often fail to take advantage of available academic resources, however, because they find that their cultural values are at odds with those that make for academic success.

WHITE REACTION

The case for white males. Daniel Seligman *Fortune* 123:107 Ja 28 '91

Robert A. Gordon, professor of sociology at Johns Hopkins, says that white males are being minoritized in discussions of the U.S. work force and economy. In other words, white males are being represented as a shrinking part of the work force, usually to buttress the argument that more affirmative action is needed to meet U.S. work force needs in the 21st century. Just because white males will no longer constitute a majority of the work force does not mean that their role should be deemphasized.

Prejudice against white students? *Newsweek* 115:78 Ap 23 '90

Fed up with what they perceive as favored treatment of blacks, some white college students are forming White Student Unions to promote white culture and pride. The unions want to eliminate affirmative action and minority scholarships. They also object to the curtailing of Eurocentric studies to make room for African and Asian studies. The unions, which have attracted few members, have so far caused little concern among campus officials or blacks.

The complexities of affirmative action. Robert J. Bresler
USA Today (Periodical) 118:7 S '89

Elected officials, not the Supreme Court, should decide whether the opportunities created by affirmative action outweigh the costs of white resentment and black stigmatization. As its rationale shifted from egalitarianism to individualism, affirmative action became increasingly controversial, angering some white males and weakening the political consensus for civil rights. In addition, it has placed an onerous stigma on minority achievement, which some people suspect of being based on race rather than on merit. There is no clear evidence that affirmative action has reduced racism, and it may even have fueled racial resentment. American legislators should give serious consideration to the side effects of affirmative action.

Testing the waters on race (quota issue). Laurence I. Barrett *Time* 136:21–2 D 24 '90

Republicans are pulling back from exploiting the quota issue. In November it appeared that President George Bush and the GOP would try to capitalize on the resentment of white voters toward programs that seem to benefit minorities unfairly. Since then, Democrats have criticized the president for fueling racial resentment and for his appeasement of Republican senator Jesse Helms, who blatantly played on the insecurity of white voters in his reelection campaign. Two events that indicate confusion in the Bush administration over the quota issue are the announcement by William Bennett, a critic of affirmative action, that he would not become GOP party chief, and the ruling of an Education Department official that most college scholarships can no longer be reserved for minorities.

Paul Johnson: in defense of the white male. Susan Faludi *Ms. Magazine* 16:65 Ja '88

Paul Johnson, who lost his promotion to dispatcher in Santa Clara County to Diane Joyce in a landmark Supreme Court ruling, believes that white males have become the scapegoats for all past discrimination in the United States. Last summer, Johnson sent a letter entitled Open Letter to the White Males of America to newspapers around the country to warn other men of the victimization they face from affirmative action. Ironically, Johnson's wife, Betty, composed and typed the letter, and it was her paycheck that made Johnson's court battle possible.